Developing Support and Allied Staff in Higher Education

Developing Support and Allied Staff in Higher Education

John Doidge, Bob Hardwick and
Jenny Wilkinson

**KOGAN
PAGE**

YOURS TO HAVE AND TO HOLD

BUT NOT TO COPY

First published in 1998

Apart from any fair dealing for the purposes of research or private study, or criticism or review, as permitted under the Copyright, Designs and Patents Act 1988, this publication may only be reproduced, stored or transmitted, in any form or by any means, with the prior permission in writing of the publishers, or in the case of reprographic reproduction in accordance with the terms and licences issued by the CLA. Enquiries concerning reproduction outside those terms should be sent to the publishers at the undermentioned address:

Kogan Page Limited
120 Pentonville Road
London N1 9JN

© Bob Hardwick, Jenny Wilkinson, John Doidge and named contributors, 1998

The right of Bob Hardwick, Jenny Wilkinson and John Doidge to be identified as authors of this work has been asserted by them in accordance with the Copyright, Designs and Patents Act 1988.

British Library Cataloguing in Publication Data

A CIP record for this book is available from the British Library.

ISBN 0 7494 2417 6

Typeset by JS Typesetting, Wellingborough, Northants.
Printed and bound in Great Britain by Clays Ltd, St. Ives plc

Contents

The contributors

John Doidge was Head of Staff Development at Nottingham Trent University until September 1997 and is now in a similar post at Aston University. He has worked extensively in the United Kingdom and abroad in staff development as a consultant in higher education and further education. He is well known for his work in quality management in organizations and has a special interest in support and allied staff development. His publications include the AUA Good Practice Guide *Total Quality Matters*, with Celia Whitchurch (1995), *Quality Teams: A Leader Guide and Workbook*, with David Bone and Bob Hardwick (1996), and 'Support and Allied Staff Developments' in *Directions in Staff Development* (ed. Angela Brew) (1995).

Professor **George Gordon** is Director of the Centre for Academic Practice at the University of Strathclyde. He served as one of the founding academic auditors with the Committee of Vice-Chancellors and Principals. He is a member of the COSHEP Staff Development Committee and has been involved in projects with the Universities' and Colleges' Staff Development Agency (UCoSDA) and the Higher Education Quality Council (HEQC). He has conducted consultancies and courses in many institutions world-wide, particularly on quality assurance, aspects of management in higher education and faculty and staff development.

Debbie Greenwood is the Senior Training and Development Officer at the University of Leeds. She has worked in personnel and staff development for 14 years in retailing, the financial sector and also as a lecturer for eight years. She is a member of the Institute of Personnel and Development and recently gained an MA in Applied Educational Studies. Her MA thesis was based on research into how support staff in universities cope with change. This led to her interest in stress prevention and control. She has also been involved in the production of two of UCoSDA's Green Papers.

Bob Hardwick is an Assistant Director at the Universities' and Colleges' Staff Development Agency (UCoSDA) and has specific responsibility for support and allied staff. He has worked in higher education for 25 years, spending the first 15 as a technician in the Department of Physics at the

University of Sheffield when he was actively involved at the local and national levels with the technicians' union MSF. He completed an MEd (Training and Development) degree in 1994 and his publications to date include *Resourceful Induction: A Training Manual for Staff in HE*, *Managing the Introduction of Appraisal for Allied/Support Staff* and *Approaches Towards the Improvement of Support/Allied Staff Development*.

Ian Hewes, after a degree in modern languages and a postgraduate certificate in education, held posts in secondary and further education for 20 years, dealing with teaching, management and the training of teachers and trainers. Along the way he acquired a diploma in film study and an MBA. He has been a Staff Development Officer at the University of Essex since 1991.

Neil Jones is Assistant Head of Personnel (Training and Development) at the University of Glamorgan. Having spent his early career in personnel and training in local government, Neil joined the then Polytechnic of Wales in 1991 to set up the staff development function from scratch. Neil seeks to combine his role as a hands-on training and development practitioner with the academic pursuits of research and scholarly activity. His professional and research interests include management development, appraisal systems and Investors in People.

Pat King is Staff Development Adviser at Kingston University. She has worked in television, merchant banking and the oil industry, joining Kingston University in 1989. Currently Pat is co-ordinating the University's pursuit of Investors in People, while pursuing an MA and an NVQ in her spare time.

Robin Middlehurst is Director of the division of Quality Enhancement of the Quality Assurance Agency. Robin has experience of teaching at all levels and joined higher education in 1986. Following postgraduate study, Robin began four years of research work at the University of Surrey into leadership and management and their development in universities. She continued researching this subject through three years of teaching, research and consultancy at the Institute of Education, culminating in the publication of *Leadership Academics* in 1993. Robin joined the HEQC in 1993 with a brief to continue her work on leadership and management in relation to higher education. Recently, Robin has worked on the Graduate Standards Programme which facilitated wide consultation with the HE sector towards the production of recommendations on assurance within HE.

Anne Sibbald is the Director of Staff Development at Heriot-Watt University. Anne has responsibility for all categories of staff but has been keenly involved in local and national programmes for support/allied staff. She has contributed to UCoSDA publications and chairs the COSHEP management sub-committee and until recently was secretary of the COHSEP administration and support staff sub-committee.

Bob Thackwray is Senior Consultant with UCoSDA, specializing in Investors in People, the evaluation of training and development, induction of new staff into higher education and equal opportunities. He is an approved and recognized Investors In People Assessor with the Assessment Network (TAN). He was formerly Head of the Centre for Educational Development at the University of Luton. He is co-author of the highly popular book *Investors in People Explained*.

Celia Whitchurch has been the Director of Strategic Development, faculty of Medicine and Dentistry at the University of Birmingham since 1992. She spent five years as Senior Planning Officer at the University of London and held faculty administrator posts at the University of Kent prior to that. She is a member of the AUA Corporate Planning Forum Steering Committee, the Editor of the AUA journal, *Perspectives*, and the author of several publications.

Jenny Wilkinson is currently the Academic Secretary for the School of Education at the University of Leicester, a role which includes responsibility for the training and development of support/allied staff within the department. Prior to that she was the Assistant Director for Staff Development with the particular remit for support and allied staff development and specialized in the provision of information technology training. She has a BEd and an MSc in computing.

Acknowledgements

We would like to thank all those many colleagues and friends who have contributed to chapters, and provided innumerable examples of good practice in institutions around the country. They are far too many to list, but we acknowledge them all.

We also want to give particular thanks to colleagues who have commented on drafts and assisted in the preparation of this text and its production. In particular, special thanks go to Ann Gretton, at Nottingham Trent University, for her patient advice and eye for detail, to families who bore the brunt of ill-temper and absence as deadlines drew near, and to Pat Lomax at Kogan Page who has been supportive throughout. And, of course, to the authors of the specialist chapters sometimes caught at a weak moment and cajoled into writing when afterwards they might have thought better of it. Well done, and thanks to all!

Introduction:
the undervalued resource

John Doidge, Bob Hardwick and Jenny Wilkinson

This book comes at a pivotal time in higher education development, and its preparation is pre-Dearing, its publication post-Dearing. However, the writing of it lies not with Dearing or any such catalyst, but more in the personal backgrounds and passionate beliefs of the authors, who wish to share with colleagues in higher education their own beliefs and experiences of the role and the dedication of the often undervalued resource – support and allied staff.

Little has been written within the higher education context about this group of staff, though in many cases they form the majority of the workforce in higher education organizations. It is also difficult to put a finger on who these people are because they range from the quasi-academics who perform research, carry out technical and teaching functions alongside teaching staff themselves, to those who support in an often unrecognized way the quality of the learning experience – cleaners, maintenance and catering staff. All of these groups, and many more, provide an important and often essential army of support to the basic learning, teaching and research function and one which higher education could not do without.

Therefore, this book is written about them and about their professional development, in a world of constantly changing pressures and priorities and diminishing resources. The name of the game is doing more, maintaining standards, retaining motivation and retraining for change.

About three years ago we were involved as organizers and teachers and trainers in the first event for developers of support staff in higher education. There are conferences and networks for academic staff developers, notably the Staff and Educational Development Association (SEDA) events, for institutional staff and educational developers events are organized by the Universities' and Colleges' Staff Development Agency (UCoSDA), and for administrators and other functional groups, eg, Association of University Administrators (AUA) and University Personnel Staff, but none for support staff developers. A group of about 25 met to consider issues concerning the development of support staff groups and to look at ways of developing the skills and knowledge of those who had responsibilities for such staff.

1

This was repeated in December 1995 in Birmingham and it struck us that some of the issues, ideas, skills, experiences and enthusiasm shared were too important to lose. Many of the contributions in this book stem from the conference itself, enhanced by insights from other colleagues who have valuable contributions to make in other areas. The unique combination the authors bring is that, collectively, they have a breadth of understanding of the nature of the subject, of its developments and a passionate belief in the importance of staff development for all. We hope that the sharing of this passion as well as the personal and practical experiences will provide not only an insight into what's going on and where, but also be inspirational, in the sense of inspiring the reader to want to know more and do more.

The book itself embraces a variety of writing styles, backgrounds and practical information and is designed to be user-friendly so that the reader can dip into passages of particular interest to them at any time. Although written before the Dearing report was published, we have set out to embrace as much as possible of the Dearing debate within the chapters themselves; hence predicting developments has been an art rather than a science, but now that we can reflect on the Dearing outcomes, our conclusions seem to have not been too wide of the mark.

It is important to be aware of some of the history of staff development when reflecting on how this book came to be written. In the mid- and late-1980s several higher education institutions were appointing staff within personnel with a responsibility for support and other staff. In the late 1980s, post-Fender report, this movement spawned the University Staff Development Unit (of the Committee of Vice-Chancellors and Principals) which subsequently has become the Universities' and Colleges' Staff Development Agency with responsibility for the overall direction of staff development policy and practice within higher education. Most higher education institutions are now members of UCoSDA, which forms a unique network of individuals with a common purpose and the ability to link with other agencies such as SEDA, AUA, etc.

Other developments have of course been crucial, including the elimination of the binary divide in 1992, and the introduction of appraisal. This latter development, beginning in 1987 with academic staff, has had a tremendous effect on the development of staff within higher education. It is both vilified and acclaimed by staff, management and trade unions within higher education, but there is no doubt its impact has been enormous, and the evidence suggests that, where it is properly applied, appraisal has been of benefit to all staff.

One of the most important of these developments has been the application of Investors in People (IIP) which has focused on standards and value for money in staff development. This and other national developments, such as National and Scottish Vocational Qualifications (N/SVQs), are so important that we have devoted separate chapters to them. Other issues such as motivation, leadership, networking, lifelong learning and flexible working are discussed in a number of chapters in the book. We have attempted to provide a logical flow through the book so that it can be read from beginning to end, and yet the reader can dip into individual chapters as they see fit.

Throughout the book we have described support and allied staff as being essential. We recognize that *all* staff within an institution are essential, but we have chosen to focus on the vital importance of this, often overlooked, group. In case there is any doubt about the essential contribution made by these people to the overall academic operations of higher education, take a moment to consider this scenario:

Imagine that you are a university or college lecturer. You arrive one morning to deliver a lecture and find that the porters have not unlocked your lecture room. When you do manage to gain entry you discover that the overhead projector and screen you requested have not been set up, but this won't matter either as in fact your lecture slides and handouts have not been prepared by the office staff. You then notice that the lecture theatre has not been cleaned and you wonder whether the students will mind sitting with yesterday's rubbish for an hour. But this should not worry you either, as there will be no students in your lecture because none of them have been registered on the course.

Without the clerical, technical and manual staff even a simple lecture would not happen. This is how essential support staff are to any academic institution.

Bob Hardwick provides a reminder of the importance of induction at every level and its link to appraisal. It is only in the last few years that universities and colleges have realized the value of introducing induction (or initial professional development) and appraisal (continuing professional development) schemes for support staff. They have still not been universally adopted but their importance is becoming obvious.

Celia Whitchurch describes the plethora of systems for quality assurance that have grown up within higher education, both nationally and locally. Her chapter explores the background, relative strengths and some experiences of institutions' approaches to quality assurance. It focuses in particular on service delivery and service statements now being developed by many institutions.

As traditional barriers between academic and support staff disappear, the role and importance of effective teams across all sectors are becoming apparent. John Doidge explores the key role that staff developers and managers have in developing, supporting and nurturing teams to become efficient and effective. One of the particular qualities of an effective team is how it applies critical thinking to problem-solving. He shares some strategies, processes and techniques which are available to teams.

One of the most important developments during the past decade has been the growth of vocationalism and N/SVQs. National training targets and N/SVQs affect universities and colleges as both employers and providers. The development of this focus on vocationalism and its link with the growth of accreditation is explored by Neil Jones and presented as an essential element of the professionalization of support services designed in part to meet the rigorous demands of efficiency and quality assurance requirements.

Pat King takes this theme further by considering the desirability of accreditation and the various types of accreditation – from in-house certificates to national accreditation schemes – that currently exist. She helps the reader to determine the strengths and weaknesses of different approaches and the relative merits of each.

The impact of new technology has been around for a long time, and it is comforting to reflect on Jenny Wilkinson's comment about the 'new technology of the electronic typewriter' in the early 1980s. Her chapter explores the impact of computerization on the work of support staff and others and discusses the response of organizations in terms of training and development.

With all this change around it is no surprise that the management of pressure and prevention of stress is an increasingly important issue, and higher education is no exception. Debbie Greenwood takes a very personal look at this issue and looks at methods that can be used by organizations, managers and individuals to manage pressure and relieve stress.

It's also too easy to forget that the career and professional development of many staff need not be linked, as it often is, to just courses and qualifications. Effective managers and staff developers are increasingly embracing new and different approaches and initiatives to staff development. Anne Sibbald examines some of the alternative activities available and explores their use and feasibility in higher education.

Bob Thackwray looks at the public national standard for staff development – Investors in People – embraced by many but achieved by few, that sets rigorous standards for staff development to use as a quality assurance framework. For those committed but not yet there, as well as for those hovering on the brink of choice and commitment, he provides a detailed prescription and checklist as a guide to meeting the national standard.

Critical in meeting all these challenges is the manager, and it would be wrong for any book on staff development to ignore the key influence of managers at each and every level. This book takes a quizzical and critical look at the development of managers in higher education. George Gordon and Robin Middlehurst explore approaches and share experiences from a number of organizations that have taken the development of managers as a cornerstone for the development of other staff.

Amongst all these developments it would be easy to lose sight of the place of the department itself, but with devolved budgeting and managerial structures placing a greater responsibility on departments in terms of identifying and delivering training and development, it is necessary to look at the way in which staff development units, or central services, can work with and support individual departments in their task. Jenny Wilkinson explores the issues involved in this.

Finally, what about the staff developer? Ian Hewes provides a personal account of the staff developer's dilemma – how to do the job and survive in today's frenetic and changing world. A cautionary tale and a challenging one, but none the less an exciting account of life as a staff developer.

We set out to write this book as a practical manual to help managers and staff developers to play their part not only in meeting the challenges of change but also acting as agents of change – helping to change the way organizations are run at the institutional, but quite crucially also, at the local level. We certainly wish to draw attention to the importance of the contribution of allied and support staff to the main aims of the organization. In the current climate of retrenchment, sombre mood and motivational crises, we hope the book is timely as a reminder of the different ways in which staff development and all that it represents can provide a motivational tool that rewards and gives recognition to staff who are quite essential to the delivery of higher education.

—1—

Induction and appraisal: vital or simply a burden?

Bob Hardwick

Straight out of school at the age of 15, my introduction to work was as an apprentice in a large engineering company in Sheffield. I duly arrived at 7.00am on my first morning armed with the only information I had received, ie a letter telling me to report to the 'Works Office'. Having found this inner sanctum, more by luck than anything else, I was asked to join my fellow first-day starters who were congregating in the corner of the factory, adjacent to the Works Office. We didn't know one another from Adam and had to stand there in full view of the rest of the workforce, as they arrived and 'clocked on'. The factory itself looked massive, although how big was difficult to estimate, as it was terribly dark and dingy. There appeared to be thousands of people arriving and suddenly a bell started ringing! A fire on my first day at work, what excitement! Alas, as we were all quickly to learn, the bell was simply to warn you that it was two minutes to seven. This was very important, as you lost money if you were more than two minutes late.

Once things had settled down, the Works Manager introduced himself and told us that someone from the training section of personnel would see us later in the morning (as they didn't start until 9.00am), and that, in the meantime, we would be allocated to one of the various sections. He proceeded to escort us to our appropriate sections where we were introduced to the foreman and informed that we should do whatever we were instructed to, but added in a very serious tone, 'Do not touch any of the machinery, as it can be very dangerous'. Induction completed!

What about the *appraisal* processes? Surely as apprentices, our views would be sought on the training provided, how our strengths could be developed, how any weaknesses might be addressed, and so on? Dream on. Not once in my five years as an apprentice was I ever asked what I would like to do. Management made all the decisions, moving us from one section to another, as they saw fit. This is not to imply that I didn't get a good basic training in engineering, but as for any meaningful dialogue between the trainees and the training office, forget it. The only time you were interviewed was if you received a poor report from the local college regarding your day release course. So, if you were lucky, at the end of five years you would receive a log book outlining the training undertaken and the qualifications obtained. You were then put to work as a turner, a miller, a grinder, a welder, an inspector, etc dependent, usually, on where there happened to be a vacancy. And still there was no appraisal process.

So how much better were things when I moved into higher education (HE) as a technician, 25 years ago? Not much. In fact my induction was probably worse, as my expectations were much higher. I could relate a very similar story to the one above but essentially induction was non-existent. As for appraisal, this took the form of an annual assessment or review of the job and had little or nothing to do with how well the individual was performing. Once again, this process was carried out by the line manager, usually without any direct contact with the individual and this did not change during my 15 years as a workshop technician.

This chapter concentrates on these two developmental activities, induction and appraisal, as they can both have a profound effect on all staff in any organization. It will examine some of the changes that have occurred over the last ten years in terms of induction and appraisal, particularly for support and allied staff, in higher education.

Induction and Initial Professional Development (IPD)

'Induction is the *Cinderella* of staff development, full of missed opportunities' (Hughes and Thackwray, 1996). Induction is not only about the first few days in a new job but it is the organization's first chance to make a lasting impression on a new member of staff. That might be something as simple as letting them know that 'we are a caring employer'. Obviously, the induction process helps to reduce the anxiety for a new member of staff but the major reasons for its importance are probably:

- it is the first phase of a career-long professional development programme;
- it reduces the time taken for a new colleague to become effective;
- it is likely to improve motivation and hence the individual's contribution to the institution and it is likely to lead to lower attrition rates;
- it explains the institution's overall mission and aims, so that the individual can see where the job fits;
- it helps develop working relationships with colleagues.

(Hardwick, 1992)

In order to achieve these goals, induction programmes will have to include all new recruits, movers, returners, redeployed personnel, etc in all the staff categories.

What is induction or Initial Professional Development (IPD)?

Starting a new job can be very stressful and although information may have been gleaned from the advertisement, the job description and the selection interview, it is often not totally clear what to expect on that first morning. This is where induction or the term that I prefer, Initial Professional Development, can be of great benefit. It should aim to make the transition to the new job as smooth and trouble-free as possible and will therefore need a planned and phased approach by management. Induction has been defined as:

> Arrangements made by, or on behalf of, management to familiarise the new employee with the working organisation, welfare and safety matters, general conditions of employment, and the work of the department or section in which s/he is employed. It is a continuous process starting from the first contact with the employer.

> (Department of Employment, 1971)

Whilst this definition is rather dated it does encapsulate the concept of IPD and takes on board the key features:

- the process is part of a professional development programme for *all* groups of staff;
- it is the initial stage in a continuing development process;
- it starts to develop the concept of life-long learning and development in the minds of both employees and employers.

IPD or induction needs to be systematic and planned in order to prevent my experiences of the process being replicated. It is no longer acceptable to place a new member of staff in the work environment and expect that, given time, they will not only master the main components of the job but will also come to terms with the complexity of the institution's goals, organization, staffing and geography. Evidence suggests that organizations which do invest time and effort in the IPD process can expect greater commitment, lower labour turnover and a more content workforce.

Higher education and induction or IPD

Most higher education institutions (HEIs) now have some form of central induction programme for new staff, although how each operates is very variable. For example, the regularity of the programmes varies from being held weekly in one HEI, whilst in others, one per year is not uncommon. Some are for academic staff only, others run one for academic staff and a separate one for support and allied staff, whilst a number of HEIs have integrated the induction process and all new staff are invited to attend, regardless of which staff group they belong to. These programmes are normally used to inform new members of staff of the organization's mission and goals but they constitute only one stage of the induction.

Other stages in the process need careful consideration and planning so that they can be delivered effectively, in a well structured manner. The style and content of the programmes and their delivery are problematical as they (particularly institutional induction) usually have to cater for a wide range of backgrounds and skills. Care should be taken to ensure that 'information overload' is eliminated from this stage of the IPD process and this can be assisted by using a variety of formats and styles. Talking at the participants for long periods is not recommended and a list of tips, adapted from Hughes and Thackwray (1996), that provides some useful suggestions, is included in Appendix A on p. 13.

It is helpful to think of the overall structure of IPD in terms of six different stages:

1. the pre-employment stage;
2. the first days;
3. introduction to and familiarization with the job;
4. introduction to and familiarization with the department or section;
5. introduction to and familiarization with the institution (outlined above);
6. the wider HE framework.

Not all these stages will be relevant to every new starter, or to particular groups of staff, but what better way to create the right early impression with the prospective starter than to at least send them an information pack? They may not need a university or college calendar at this stage but some 'light' pre-work reading and an insight into the organization might be just the thing to gear them up for those difficult first few days.

The way forward

Many HEIs have progressed significantly in terms of IPD for new staff over the last ten years but still have some way to go for staff returning to the work place and those changing their jobs. Effective IPD is no more or less than a function of good management and should be seen as an integral and important duty of all those who have staff reporting to them. Some managers in HE still need to be convinced or persuaded that giving more time to the IPD process will have real benefits for staff, their departments and the institution. One avenue that some HEIs adopt, mainly for academic staff, is the appointment of a mentor to each new starter. This is someone who, on a one-to-one basis, is available to offer advice, coaching and assistance, usually at the job or departmental IPD stages. This system could certainly be extended to support and allied staff.

IPD needs to be viewed as an entitlement for all new members of staff and this consequently puts the onus on managers (at all levels) to organize the delivery of and participation in programmes. The key message is that IPD should be built into the operational strategy and management of the organization, leading on to a range of related and complementary activities, such as appraisal.

Appraisal: dreaded or not?

Background

Even that simple question would be met by a multitude of responses from HE staff, ranging from 'definitely' to 'staff would be very upset if they were denied this opportunity'. Why, in the late 1990s, does HE still have this marked disparity about a process which is readily accepted outside the sector as being an effective way of involving staff in their own career development? One reason might be the word itself. As Hardwick and Greenwood (1993) wrote, 'appraisal has sadly had the effect of striking fear and trepidation into the minds of allied staff . . .'. There are, of course, other, probably more understandable, reasons including the following:

- it takes up far too much valuable time;
- it can damage departmental relationships;
- it increases the power of authoritarian managers;
- it can reveal deficiencies which are difficult to rectify;
- it is treated with varying degrees of seriousness;
- it can undermine the goodwill factor.

Another reason for appraisal not being universally welcomed by HE is the way it was originally introduced for academic staff in the late 1980s as a condition attached to a salary increase. This did nothing to assist its acceptance by staff and although the schemes for technical and secretarial staff were not generally introduced until the 1990s, the stigma still remained. Even now, only about 40 per cent of HEIs have appraisal schemes in place for support and allied staff and this figure drops to less than 15 per cent for manual and ancillary staff. Obviously, progress is slow and the current financial position of a number of universities and colleges does not help, but a significant and growing number of support staff do now have access to an appraisal or career review scheme.

The important task, now, is how to build on this and work towards the position where staff appraisal is commonplace throughout the system. This situation, however desirable, will be difficult to achieve. Having been involved over the last few years in the training of appraisers and appraisees, I was surprised to learn that many staff do not fully understand what appraisal is, how it operates, and what its aims and benefits are, etc. This is yet another obstacle to its mass availability sector-wide.

Appraisal in HE: aims and benefits

During my 15 years as a university technician, not once was I ever asked, 'How are you doing? Can we do anything to help?' The process itself should be a means of encouraging reflection on a regular basis. It is not a 'one-off' event and needs to occur at regular intervals (at least annually). It should also be systematic, which will require a common set of procedures or guidelines to be in place, meaning that the scheme should be operated in a uniform and harmonious manner throughout the organization.

The initial procedures should lead to an extended interview. I deliberately use the word extended because it should not be, as one person described it to me recently, 'two minutes and it was all over'. On investigating further I found this to be an accurate account of the individual's appraisal interview and, needless to say, it left the person concerned totally disillusioned with the whole process. Whilst no definitive time can be given for the interview (on average they probably last about an hour), the criterion must be that the appraisee feels that they have had a reasonable input into the appraisal discussion. The interview can be fairly informal and create the opportunity for open discussion to take place between the appraisee and the appraiser on a range of issues which might include:

- job performance;
- capabilities and competences;
- future potential;
- the setting of future objectives;
- developmental needs;
- impediments to development.

This list serves to demonstrate that the discussion can be wide-ranging and should be structured to allow both parties an adequate input. The outcome usually includes a number of action points or targets for the coming period and should be aimed at building and developing the individual's strengths as well as addressing any weaknesses that might have been identified. In order to achieve a satisfactory outcome the aims of appraisal need to be clearly understood and the following list, adapted from *Staff Appraisal in Higher Education: The Key to Effective Implementation* (Partington *et al.*, 1990), encapsulates the main points:

- increasing the job satisfaction of staff;
- maintaining and improving existing high standards of performance;
- improving motivation and morale;
- identifying and developing staff capabilities and competences which in turn might enhance potential for promotion;

- improving staff performance;
- imparting knowledge to staff of institutional, departmental and sectional goals and exploring their part in the achievement of them;
- assisting with the adaptation to change.

As with IPD, effective appraisal simply means having sound management procedures in place. First, staff and their representative bodies, which for support and allied staff is usually the recognized trade union, need to feel a sense of ownership of the appraisal scheme. They need to know that it has senior management support, how it will operate in practice, what safeguards have been built in to the scheme and what the benefits are. Second, staff need some assurances in terms of training provision before the scheme is introduced. Appraiser training should, in my view, be compulsory but it is just as important to provide adequate training to appraisees. I like the approach that offers the same training to all those included in a particular scheme. Mixing appraisers and appraisees on the same training programme can be very helpful in demonstrating that everyone will be provided with the same information about the scheme and how it will operate. Finally, and very importantly, the interview needs to take the form of a dialogue between the two parties. If this part of the process becomes a one sided management monologue then its effectiveness will be diminished and the scheme will quickly fall into disrepute. Ownership, training and dialogue are therefore critical components of any scheme. Even with all these in place, staff will still ask, 'What's in it for me?'

There still appears to be a fairly widespread distrust and healthy disregard for anything new that management wish to introduce. Staff can usually see the benefits of appraisal for the organization: a means of better identifying training needs; improvements in communication; linking departmental and organizational needs; an opportunity to co-ordinate various activities; and an interchange of ideas leading to a more open style of management. Why, then, do staff invariably struggle when asked to identify what the benefits might be for them? There is no simple answer but it could once again boil down to the manager's own approach to explaining and sharing with staff the benefits that should accrue. Here is a list which I regularly use as a handout at appraisal training sessions. The benefits to staff should be:

- a regular opportunity to talk about their achievements, difficulties and future development;
- a clearer understanding of their responsibilities and how these relate to the goals and functions of the department and the institution as a whole;
- participation in the setting of priorities and the shaping of their own career development;
- formal acknowledgement and appreciation of their abilities and achievements and thereby increased job satisfaction and motivation;

- identification of areas of difficulty and weakness within a framework of constructive openness and accessible provision of practical help to overcome these difficulties;
- more accurate perceptions of colleagues' roles, responsibilities, competences and capabilities.

(Partington *et al.*, 1990)

Conclusion

Knowing what appraisal is, what its aims are, what benefits can derive from it, and what processes and procedures will be incorporated to ensure its effectiveness would, I am convinced, go a long way to persuading staff of its undoubted merits. Introducing appraisal needs:

- the visible support of senior management;
- a certain amount of resourcing (both time and money);
- training of appraisees and appraisers prior to the scheme's launch;
- ownership of the scheme shared between management and staff;
- appraisers (managers) ensuring that action plans and targets are realistic, attainable and adequately resourced.

If IPD and appraisal become the norm in HEIs, then we could very quickly see a marked change in the culture of our organizations throughout the sector. Continuing professional development (CPD) would be enhanced for all staff; organizational, as well as staff and educational, development would be to the fore; we would move towards the learning organization model; and the concept of lifelong learning would be embraced. We need to dispel the idea that training and developing staff are a burden. IPD and appraisal are vital and could jointly form the catalyst required to unlock so much potential across the sector which has been left untapped for too many support and allied staff.

Appendix A: ways of enlivening IPD programmes

- Use an icebreaker to get people talking. For example, at the induction session, ask your new staff to talk to as many people as they can and find one thing they have in common with each other at a personal level and at a job-related level. This encourages discussion and shows the diversity of people in the institution.
- Token prizes can be awarded at certain stages to encourage networking, teamwork and competition in a light-hearted way but in the spirit of active learning. If you have corporate gifts – pens, etc – so much the better.

- Show a video on fire and/or theft prevention. Much of the rest of the safety information may be departmentally specific.
- Find out from the Safety Department the main causes of accidents to new staff and highlight these.
- Show a video about how the main departments function.
- Lead a discussion on customer care.
- Include the students' views in your organization.
- Organize a visit to an IT area to view the World Wide Web.
- Towards the end of the central induction programme, arrange a summary discussion in groups on what they still need to know, and tap into the self-help available.
- Invite more experienced people to join the groups in the above discussions, as they consider the things they still need to know.
- Run a 'question time' discussion as the final session.
- Get a spokesperson to ask the questions on behalf of the groups (this makes them anonymous and thus less daunting).
- Get someone to give a talk on 'A day in the life of' an academic; a technician; a porter, etc.
- Get someone who was 'new last year' to give their impressions, or the things they have learnt.
- Do a quick questionnaire to recent starters on 'three things I wish I'd known when I started'. Produce a question and answer list.
- Provide a talk on equal opportunities with a video.
- Do a case study on equal opportunities and progress within the institution.
- Lead a discussion on what they need to know about Control of Substances Hazardous to Health (COSHH). How will they find out? How will they record it?
- Play a game to describe the university structures, using blu-tac and laminated names of departments, committees and senior staff. This shows the variety of perceptions – but is there a right answer? (You need to be able to help – you didn't get them together to exchange ignorance!)
- Use an Open Learning Centre. Some organizations are developing CD-ROM to provide a tailored introduction to their institution. If that's too expensive why not use books and text and World Wide Web to structure an IT induction?
- Get them to work on action plans. At some stage towards the end of the day, get the participants to sit and think, on their own and then with another person, just what they are now going to do to increase their learning: 'I have learned about xxx and I need to find out more about yyy.'
- Arrange reunions of those who have attended central induction. This should show your commitment to excellent customer care and provide a chance for you to hear about all the things that they now wish you had included in their induction process. Such sessions seem to be

particularly popular if scheduled for early to mid-December.

- Provide a handbook for new staff. This can have blank spaces in it to serve as reminders of the things they need to find out for themselves, such as fire exits. It should have blanks for the action plans mentioned above.
- Provide an introduction to the appraisal processes.
- Offer an introduction to the promotions and rewards procedures.
- Attend someone else's induction, and then. . .
- Invite them to yours!
- Run a quiz or a treasure hunt, working in mixed groups, to find out the answers to a series of questions, eg how do you book a squash court, what is the name of the Chancellor?

References

Department of Employment (1971) *Glossary of Training Terms*, 2nd edn, London: HMSO.

Hardwick, RC (1992) *Resourceful Induction: A Manual of Materials for Higher Education*, UCoSDA/ESSO, Sheffield.

Hardwick, RC and Greenwood, D (1993) *Managing the Introduction of Appraisal for Allied/Support Staff*, Occasional Green Paper No 4, UCoSDA, Sheffield.

Hughes, P and Thackwray, B (1996) *The Staff Developer and Induction*, SEDA/UCoSDA Staff Development Paper No 2, UCoSDA, Sheffield.

Partington, PA *et al.* (1990) *Staff Appraisal in Higher Education: The Key to Effective Implementation: a Knowledge/Skills Training Package*, UCoSDA/CVCP, Sheffield.

2

Quality assurance and service delivery

Celia Whitchurch

Very often the first step to quality improvement is the airing of problems and the sharing of difficulties.

(Robin Middlehurst, *HEQC Update*, September 1996)

Context

The increased market orientation of the UK higher education system, driven over the last ten years by Funding Council formulae and a continuous reduction of the unit of resource, has led to a focus on students, funding agencies and employers as customers for universities' outputs. This has been accompanied by a doubling in the size of the system since 1988 and much greater diversity of programmes and institutional missions.

Institutions are therefore striving to establish and sustain a market niche and competitive advantage. Providing what the customer wants, rather than what the institution thinks they should want, has assumed a much higher priority than hitherto. In order to capture and maintain their market share of students and resources, institutions are increasingly concerned with outcomes, service delivery, and the quality standards required to sustain and improve their position. Critical to achieving these goals are staff performance and attitudes, particularly the ability to anticipate and manage change so as to maximize market opportunities and attract business, be it for teaching and learning, research, technology transfer or other spin-off activity.

External systems

Quality assurance as it relates to UK higher education could be said to have been formally 'invented' by the Reynolds Committee on Academic Standards in 1987. Following on from that it was formalized by the procedures required by the Higher Education Funding Councils (HEFC) and the Higher Education Quality Council (HEQC), creating an explicit focus for academic outcomes and performance. However, the confidence of funding agencies and the consumers of teaching and research can only be maintained if academic support systems are able to monitor and develop their standards effectively. Some institutions have introduced internal administrative and management audits that may include value-for-money studies and benchmarking comparisons with other institutions. This top-down approach at institutional level must, if it is to work, be matched by a bottom-up approach from individual managers to develop the potential of their staff and to obtain maximum performance from them. While quality audit and quality assurance originally focused on monitoring, measuring and rectifying shortcomings, current thinking tends towards quality enhancement, ie, the identification and development of good practice individually and collectively which can be shared within and between institutions.

The HEQC's Quality Enhancement Group defined its role as 'supporting institutional and departmental self-regulation by enhancing the capacity for critical self-reflection at both levels [institutional and departmental] of an institution' (HEQC, 1996). Managers may wish to think about taking these concepts on board in relation to their own teams. The HEQC Quality Enhancement Group saw enhancement as complementing audit and assurance: 'the key features of "pure" quality enhancement are the promotion and stimulation of worthwhile educational development and change which is either unrelated or only loosely related to an "account-ability" framework'. The Group's completion of departmental case studies *Managing for Quality* (HEQC, 1995b) identified the development of managerial capability, particularly managing change, as a critical factor in quality strategies at departmental level.

The Higher Education Funding Council for England's quality assessment grades include a 'quality assurance and enhancement' cell, and the Higher Education Quality Council has, in its Graduate Standards Programme (HEQC, 1995a), established a number of projects centred on best practice, including internal audit, modularity and curriculum frameworks, external examining and professional body accreditation, together with regional seminars mounted as part of their Quality Assurance and Enhancement Network. The process of enhancement involves both analysis and reflection on information emerging from the accountability process, as well as a dialogue about innovative thinking. The emphasis on self-evaluation and improvement means that it involves everyone, not just institutional heads.

A report by the HEQC on the use of internal audit defines the essential purpose of an audit as being 'to check and verify that responsibility for quality standards is being fully discharged and that the means for doing so are effective, and to identify areas for improvement and continuing professional development by stimulating self-critical reflection' (HEQC, 1997). The developmental aspect looks essentially at strengths, weaknesses and potential. The principles can be incorporated into staff development and appraisal at all levels.

The new Quality Assurance Agency for Higher Education was established in March 1997 with the aim of harmonizing internal and external review arrangements, avoiding duplication and overlap, accommodating a wide range of structures, and managing a series of external reviews (HEFCE/CVCP, 1996). The first Chief Executive, John Randall, in an early interview expressed the view that

> We have to be seen as more than an organisation that comes round and tells people what they are not getting right. We have to be an organisation that is interested in promoting good practice, and giving examples of that which is best. . . It's about benchmarking, looking for areas where you can learn from the experience of others. It's positive in the sense of identifying areas for improvement.
>
> (HEFCE, 1997)

The ability to produce the right goods and services of the right quality, at the right price, at the right time was emphasized in the series of Government White Papers on Competitiveness (1991, 1994, 1995, 1996) that promoted enterprise as a factor in the success of UK public sector operations and encouraged a culture of innovation, with continuous improvements in performance and productivity. The 1994 White Paper is very specific that one of the critical factors in all this is the development of staff to achieve new skills and effectiveness, to be comfortable with learning and change, and to create a sense of partnership with customers, suppliers, investors and the community. A constant interface with others, inside and outside the institution, requires mental agility and the ability to digest, analyse and regenerate information in an appropriate form and at an appropriate time.

Quality management systems applied to the workplace

Promoting the quality of institutional services is likely to involve a combination of a systems approach (the McKinsey 'Hard S's' of management – structures, strategies and systems) and a people-oriented approach (the 'soft S's' – staff, style, shared values and skills) (Pascale and Athos, 1982). The external quality assurance scrutiny to which all institutions are subject tends towards the systematic, audit trail approach, checking gaps or oversights in provision. For internal purposes such a blueprint can help to ensure consistency, that nothing goes by default, that links and cross-working (particularly in multidisciplinary activities) are not neglected. It does, however, lay emphasis on the inspectorial rather than the improvement end of the quality spectrum. It provides assurance and accountability to funders and customers in the form of continuous assessment (regular monitoring) and periodic 'examinations' or reviews. In many cases it has led to the establishment of more stringent internal review mechanisms pointing up current problems, strengths, weaknesses and institutional priorities. However, the current plethora of quality structures and procedures has been criticized for fragmenting consideration of institutional activities and outputs, rather than capturing the synergy of the whole as a corporate enterprise.

The individual manager, while using these mechanisms as part of the toolkit, may therefore be more convinced by the 'appointing good people and letting them get on with it' school of thought. Somewhere in between is the idea that service delivery depends on individuals, often working in teams, and that developing them is likely to provide a solid basis for continued success as measured by systems. In the IMHE Project, Quality Management, Quality Assessment and the Decision-Making Process, currently at the stage of final analysis, it is emerging that 'At both system and institutional levels, factors such as trust and personal relationships seem to be as important as structures and processes' (Brennan, 1996). Brennan has also suggested (1995) that a system which produces public summative judgements is likely to lead to responses geared to 'outwit' the assessors rather than a genuine concern for improvement.

The harnessing of continuous improvement and enhancement at the level of the individual employee is the foundation of a number of well known management techniques, including Total Quality Management and Business Process Engineering, as well as the Investors in People Initiative. These approaches focus on the customer, customer care and service delivery, as well as getting the best out of staff, essentially by making jobs more rewarding and generating corporate commitment. Comfort with flexibility and change is an essential part of all three management philosophies, together with a momentum for improvement and learning for individuals and the institution. Margins of success or failure in terms of quality, resources and competitive advantage are so tight these days that institutions cannot afford to neglect growth opportunities for their existing stock of person power. To do otherwise is likely to mean downsizing of their human resource, since investment in people is their major financial commitment. Total Quality Management (TQM) uses techniques such as group working through quality improvement teams and quality circles to solve specific problems or suggest improvements to existing practices, and thus raise the general level of service delivery. These teams use methodologies which range from brainstorming, cause and effect diagrams, critical success factors and processes and statistical techniques. These are set out in more detail in the AUA Good Practice Guide *Total Quality Matters* (Doidge and Whitchurch, 1993).

Advocates of Business Process Re-engineering (BPR) (sometimes referred to as Business Re-engineering or just Re-engineering) would argue that TQM fosters continual improvement of existing tasks, structures and outcomes, without looking at the opportunities provided by fundamental re-design of processes. BPR aims to recreate coherent and cross-functional working methods that have been fragmented and flawed by division of labour, bureaucracy, assumptions about necessary sequences of activity, or incremental growth of non-value-added work. Again, the focus is on delivery as it impacts on the customer, aiming to provide a single point of contact with someone in the organization who has the ability to make decisions (Hammer and Champy, 1993). Quality is enhanced by encouraging staff to look for imaginative solutions which might then be applied to problems that arise, as well as creating new possibilities.

Investors in People is the subject of another chapter of this book. The correlation between institutional achievement of the National Standard for Effective Investment in People with service delivery is the linking of staff development to institutional objectives. When institutions fail to attain the standard it is usually because corporate objectives are not well enough embedded in individual management practices, because understanding and beliefs 'on the ground' do not reflect written statements or plans, or because resource commitments are insufficient to achieve intended outcomes. Through public commitment to objectives, planning and implementation of staff development processes and evaluation of outcomes, institutions seeking the standard are expected to raise standards of quality, improve employee motivation and customer satisfaction, and enhance their reputation externally. Managers are expected to understand and develop the skills and knowledge needed to achieve institutional targets, and to close gaps where necessary. Good communication, cascading to all levels of the institution, is of the essence, and is tested and verified by assessors.

Some quality promoting strategies

What can be done in-house? A number of 'good practice' methods have been adopted not only to promote robust management processes but also to link them to quality outcomes. They can be used by individual managers at the sub-institutional level, possibly in combination with some of the quality systems described above. An awareness among users (internal and external) of expected service, its likely costs, and comparisons through, for instance, benchmarking and market testing, reflects on the overall health of the service provider.

Service level statements are becoming increasingly common between the providers of services (such as the library, registry, estates office, catering) and internal and external customers. They usually aim to specify the nature of the service, with timing, frequency, quality and costs to match the needs of customers. In the case of services to students, the statements are likely to link into a university's student charter, if it has one. A service level statement specifies agreed standards and targets in relation to the impact of the services on the customer (eg expected response and waiting times, staff attitudes, complaints procedures). It also outlines any expected obligation on the part of the customer (for instance, to return books within a certain period to the library), the basis or formula on which charging takes place (eg pay-as-you-go or based on historic patterns of usage) and caveats such as external circumstances which would affect the service's ability to deliver. The duration of the agreement, timetable for review and procedures for settling disputes, compensation for failure to perform and performance measures would be built in. A list of the qualitative and quantitative elements that might be included in a statement is shown below.

- nature and quality of service to be provided;
- service provider and service user obligations and reciprocal arrangements;
- duration of the agreement and timetable for review;
- frequency of service delivery;
- basis of charging;
- performance criteria or measurement;
- procedure for settling disputes;
- remedies for failure to perform or deliver.

When preparing a service level statement it is helpful to remember the following steps based on the British Standard ISO 9002 for quality management:

- define what you do;
- state who your clients and customers are;
- say how you evaluate what you do and describe quality assurance mechanisms;
- state operational objectives within the context of overall strategic objectives;
- establish what standards you are aiming to meet and what standards you expect of your customers;
- state the expected constraints on meeting these standards;
- indicate proposed service improvements (with timetable if possible).

Establishing standards in this way helps to ensure quality outcomes through reduction of time lost through errors, duplication or repetition of work. Part of the process necessitates staff being fully aware of their roles and responsibilities, being clear about the expectations made about them, and receiving the necessary training to carry out the tasks required.

Formal academic quality assurance processes demand a review of support facilities and services, and, as a corollary to this, some institutions have developed an internal management/administrative audit of service units, to ensure that they are reinforcing the academic enterprise in the most appropriate and cost-effective way. Such a review might take place every five years or so and would be likely to include a statement and assessment of objectives, a consideration of appropriate performance indicators against stated objectives, and perhaps most important, the evaluation of customer feedback. As with individual appraisal systems, such reviews should be conducted in a non-threatening manner, enabling desirable change to be achieved where required through a constructive exchange between the review team and members of the unit.

Good practice indicates that the review team should include an external member or members, for instance, a lay member of Council or person from another university. The process is likely to involve some kind of self-assessment document, with questions to guide the unit's response, and suggestions about additional material that might be submitted (see below for possible types of question). Areas covered may well include:

- the role of the unit in relation to the institution as a whole;
- objectives or structure or resourcing of the unit;
- the contribution made by unit staff;
- customer or user perceptions;
- monitoring and evaluation of the unit's activities or performance indicators;
- improvement strategies.

The following are examples of the types of question used in a self-assessment document.

- describe the objectives and activities of the section or unit being assessed in the context of institutional aims, objectives and plans;
- how are priorities identified?;
- describe the organizational structure of the section or unit and how this contributes to the achievement of its objectives;
- how are activities monitored and reviewed and what performance indicators are used?;
- how are resources (including space) allocated and expenditure controlled against the section's budget?;
- describe the use made of Information Systems (IS) and how this enhances operations;
- how does the section or unit interact with other sections of the institution and contribute to corporate strategy?;
- what are the main problems facing the section and how are they being addressed?;
- what are the main constraints (internal and external) facing the section?;

- how does the section communicate and interact with its users or customers?;
- how do the roles of individual members of staff contribute to the above?;
- what arrangements exist for the professional development of staff?

Helpful additional material might include an organization chart, with names of staff and individuals' responsibilities, a process diagram showing the operation of systems and critical paths, a budget forecast for the next year and an analysis of performance against the previous year, as well as quantitative and qualitative feedback from users, if this has been collected. A user survey, including face-to-face discussions with users, may also be part of the review.

There should be at least one meeting between the review team and unit members, with one at an early stage to set the parameters and highlight any areas or issues that are considered particularly significant. A visit to the unit by the review team is also likely to be an important component of the process.

Institutions will have their own views about how widely internal audit reports should be disseminated, in addition to members of the unit concerned. For instance, it may be regarded as a useful piece of management information for the institutional planning committee. As with individual appraisals, it should focus on development and enhancement issues, while addressing strengths and weaknesses as honestly as possible. For instance, it may take a formal review to identify where 'mission drift' has occurred, or where activities or ways of undertaking them are no longer appropriate to users' current needs or expectations. It should therefore be regarded as a constructive, yet reflective process. As with appraisal, there should not be too many surprises – if there are, it may point to shortcomings in terms of communication, self-awareness, or understanding of objectives and plans.

Follow-up action of any necessary change should be undertaken by the institution's chief administrative officer in consultation with the head of the unit, and a report made to the university body which has overall responsibility for the process (such as the planning committee).

Benchmarking and market testing are useful accompaniments to the audit process as they provide markers as to whether best quality and value-for-money are being achieved (and indicate the efforts made to ensure this). External benchmarking at national level for academic activity occurs not only through the funding council research and teaching quality assessment exercises, but also through HESA's annual volumes of statistics (HESA, 1996a, b and c). The problem with broad indicators provided at national level is that they do not always compare like with like, and therefore their validity and meaning are not always readily apparent. Some institutions have found that more reliable measures can be achieved by grouping together studies of specific areas such as management of information services, residences, or catering provision, through which ways of achieving efficiencies and greater effectiveness can be identified. Support facilities are a particularly good area in which to do this, because universities are not in direct competition in providing them, as they are in relation to teaching, research, or technology transfer. It is therefore easier to achieve collaborative partnership in the interests of good practice.

Market testing (or competitive tendering) for services has a similar purpose, giving users the opportunity to contract with external providers for services if these prove to be of better value than those provided internally. Obvious candidates for testing include discrete, self-standing functions such as security, cleaning, catering, maintenance and waste disposal. Others might include (as has happened quite widely in local government) internal audit, pension administration and legal services. Institutions do, however, need to be clear that they are able to discharge their legal obligations and to meet acceptable quality standards through any external providers.

Fostering individual development

There have been a number of moves to define the desirable capabilities and competencies in employees in order for them to contribute effectively to the future economic, social and cultural life of the organization. A Department for Education and Employment and Cabinet Office Skills Audit (DFEE, 1996) used multinational companies to identify the key skills of good written and oral communication, numeracy, facility with IT, personal effectiveness, teamworking, problem-solving, and the capacity to extend learning throughout life. The Enterprise in Higher Education programme had earlier addressed the extent to which transferable skills, such as IT and languages, managing change, decision-making and entrepreneurship could be incorporated and assessed within higher education programmes of study. The HEQC's Graduate Standards Programme (HEQC, 1995a), likewise, is seeking to identify core competencies – these are likely to extend the list to include traditional intellectual skills such as synthesis and evaluation of knowledge, critical analysis, reflective practice and creative thought. Managers may wish to draw up their own list of competencies, as well as undertaking a skills audit, in order to identify gaps and, through the appraisal and staff development process, formulate a plan for closing them. Involving members of the team in this process would help to inculcate self-awareness and ownership, individually and corporatively.

Learning has been described (MacFarlane, 1994) as 'a dialogue between imagination and experience'. It takes place through phases – preparing to tackle relevant material, acquiring the necessary information, relating it to previous knowledge, transforming and interpreting it by establishing organizational frameworks, and developing personal understanding (CSUP, 1992). This provides a firm basis for improving the quality of performance through staff development using problem-solving techniques to establish a 'can do' environment (see Chapter 3 on teams, team working and problem-solving). An individual's ability to learn, analyse and reconstruct depends on building on blocks of knowledge and skills in relation to discrete aspects of the environment with which they are familiar, for instance, the immediate workplace. This can be termed a 'microworld' (MacFarlane, 1994). From this understanding an individual constructs their own personal 'macroworld' from a series of microworlds (Quine and Ullian, 1978). The active manager seeking to maximize the potential of his or her staff will, therefore, be well advised to foster personal responsibility in individuals to consolidate and extend their learning experiences.

The concept of a learning organization, which fosters individual and organizational development, has gained currency in the 1990s (ESRC, 1994; Senge, 1992; Argyris, 1992; Rist and Joyce, 1995). In particular, double loop learning (Senge, 1992) 'exposes underlying norms, assumptions and objectives, questioning in an effort to reformulate them into innovative and creative responses to organisational problems'. This approach enables the organization to adapt to rapid change in the environment. A prerequisite is the role of leaders in creating and committing to learning modes so as to establish an appropriate culture, since 'individuals require confidence in their ability to undertake lifelong learning and adapt to the new technologies' (ESRC, 1994). Analytical dialogue between institutional leaders and line managers about the assumptions underlying policy formation is also a key factor. However, the outcome of this dialogue must thereafter be translated by line managers using the capabilities of individuals and teams at unit and corporate levels to implement policy objectives.

Harnessing and developing the strengths of individuals to meet institutional or unit goals thus require a strong affirmation from line managers, particularly in the encouragement of innovation and enterprise. Goals need to be clearly stated in plans at all levels, as well as ways in which staff will contribute to the plan's achievement. The contribution of individuals can then be identified and monitored through the appraisal system. Good practice suggests that individuals should provide their own objectives for the forthcoming year, and link these specifically to unit objectives. Discussion can then take place as to whether or not they have been met, and if not, why not. Development initiatives can include conventional training, in-house or externally, as well as secondments to business or industry and opportunities to undertake consultancy. Exposing staff to the outside world may help to import some good ideas, and also reaffirm outward-looking attitudes. Human resource development can thus be worked into local plans in a continuous way, and be evaluated in terms of enhanced competence and productivity against goals.

Conclusion

This chapter has described a number of tools at the manager's disposal for designing and achieving quality processes and appropriate service delivery. Issues associated with performance as measured by external (customer) perceptions, and working backwards to (literally) reform internal processes where necessary, can provide a dimension which opens up possibilities such as more lateral, outcome-oriented working. Staff involvement in identifying and defining what needs to be done in a rapidly changing environment creates less certainty, but more opportunity. Achieving comfort with these new dimensions and using them to maximum effect is one of higher education managers' greatest challenges.

References

Argyris, C (1992) *On Organisational Learning*, Blackwell, Oxford.

Brennan, J (1995) *Authority, Legitimacy and Change: The Rise of Quality Assessment in Higher Education*, Centre for Educational Research and Innovation, Programme of Institutional Management in Higher Education, Paris.

Brennan, J (1996), *IMHE Information Issue 2*, Programme on Institutional Management in Higher Education, OECD, Paris.

Competing for Quality (1991) Cmnd 1730, HMSO, London.

Competitiveness: Helping Business to Win (1994) Cmnd 2563, HMSO, London.

Competitiveness: Forging Ahead (1995) Cmnd 2867, HMSO, London.

Competitiveness: Creating the Enterprise Centre of Europe (1996) Cmnd 3300, HMSO, London.

CSUP (Committee of Scottish University Principals) Working Party (1992) *Teaching and Learning in an Expanding Higher Education System*, COSHEP, Edinburgh.

CVCP (1986) *Academic Standards in Universities* (Report of the Academic Standards Group chaired by Professor P.A. Reynolds), CVCP, Sheffield.

Department for Education and Employment/Cabinet Office (1996) *Skills Audit*, HMSO, London.

Doidge, J and Whitchurch, C (1993) *Total Quality Matters*, AUA Good Practice Guide, AUA, Manchester.

ESRC (1994) *Research Specification for the ESRC: 'Learning Society: Knowledge and Skills for Employment Programme'*, ESRC, Swindon.

Hammer, M and Champy, J (1993) *Re-engineering the Corporation*, Nicholas Brealey, London.

HEFCE/CVCP Joint Planning Group for Quality Assurance in Higher Education, (September 1996) *Final Report*, HEFCE/CVCP, Bristol.

HEFCE (1997) *Council Briefing No. 9*, HEFCE, Bristol.

HESA (1996a) *Students in Higher Education Institutions 1994/95*, HESA, Cheltenham.

HESA (1996b) *Resources of Higher Education Institutions 1994/95*, HESA, Cheltenham.

HESA (1996c) *First Destinations of Students leaving Higher Education Institutions 1994/95*, HESA, Cheltenham.

HEQC (1995a) *Graduate Standards Programme, Interim Report*, HEQC, London.

HEQC (1995b) *Managing for Quality: Stories and Strategies*, HEQC, London.

HEQC (1996) *Quality Enhancement within the HEQC 1995–96*, HEQC, London.

HEQC (1997) *Report on Use of Internal Audit*, HEQC, London.

MacFarlane, AGJ (1994) *Future Patterns of Teaching and Learning*, Paper delivered to AUA Corporate Planning Forum, November.

Middlehurst, R (1996), 'Quality Enhancement', *HEQC Update*, September, London.

Pascale, R T and Athos, A G (1982) *The Art of Japanese Management*, Penguin, Harmondsworth.

Quine, W V and Ullian, J S (1978), *The Web of Belief*, Random House, New York.

Rist, R C and Joyce, M K (1995) 'Qualitative Research and Implementation Evaluation: A Path to Organisational Learning', *International Journal of Educational Research* vol. 23, no. 22, pp. 107–90.

Senge, P (1992) *The Fifth Discipline: Art and Practice of the Learning Organisation*, Century Books, London.

—3—

Teams, team working and problem-solving

John Doidge

The role of teams and team development

Organisations are about people working together and, therefore, developing effective teams must be a prime responsibility of all who manage or lead groups of people.

(Mike Woodcock, 1989)

It has long been acknowledged that the strongest organizations are built on a sense of team working and team commitment which enables them to gain the advantage of shared objectives, working purposefully together and sharing the joy of success. It can become rather clichéd but one is inevitably drawn back to the example of the football team, where it has long been held, and I suppose amply demonstrated, that a well coached and motivated team will often beat a team of gifted individuals who do not know how to work together.

Universities are full of teams and depend on them effectively working together in order to get things done as part of the responsibilities involved in delivering and supporting teaching, learning and research. It is always possible, though some would claim that the sense of team working may not always be appropriate. I have often come across debate within universities where individual teachers or researchers, and indeed other professionals, have argued that they work on their own, develop themselves and nothing can be gained from working with others. However, it is unlikely that any individual can exist entirely without the help of others who, in some way, bring about what they are seeking to achieve. It is this sense of shared responsibilities and support for each other which I have spent many years trying to engender amongst all sorts of groups and at every level in organizations.

One of the most important initiatives to emerge in recent years is Investors in People (see Chapter 9) that has placed enormous emphasis on organizations behaving as teams. Indeed, several of the criteria specifically relate to aspects of team working, including shared understanding of objectives at every level and, perhaps most important of all, effective communication throughout an organization.

Teams and quality enhancement activities

Chapter 2 has described the institutional and operational requirements and strategies which influence current quality activities. Organizations have developed various approaches to quality enhancement, but some of the most effective have been in developing the link between quality enhancement and team working. Much of the thinking has been borrowed from the work in the 1950s and 1960s in Japan by American gurus (notably Deming and Juran). They placed responsibility on all employees for improving the quality of their work, and therefore products and services. During the 1980s these ideas began to take hold in the public sector and within higher education interest grew in the late 1980s in adopting and adapting these ideas. This has been especially successful in the support and service areas through use of quality improvement teams and quality circles. I shall say more about this as both technique and practice later.

I was also involved from the late 1980s onwards with the quality improvement movement and in particular saw the work and effectiveness of team working demonstrated throughout industry and the public sector. The National Society for Quality Through Team Working is an independent voluntary membership organization of charitable status of over 400 organizations offering continuous improvement training and support throughout the UK. Each is dedicated to the aim of people's involvement in product, process and service improvement. The Society provides a system of regional networks and support, annual national forums and quality and team working awards which are replicated around the world. This powerful movement for team working and quality enhancement has influenced and often led the debate in organizations of how to build in process and product improvement and at the core of their thinking has been the use of teams and team working. The principle of quality enhancements as goals has become widespread in business and industry with a particular focus emerging during the 1980s through total quality management, ISO9000 (formerly BS5750) and latterly through the quality assessment processes in higher education.

Quality teams

The notion of team working focused on the use of quality teams for quality improvement in the 1980s and 1990s. Much has been written about these approaches to collective problem-solving and enhancement activities and continuous improvement. There are certainly a number of different ways of approaching the activity ranging from the management-led, top-down approach to the grass-roots involvement and empowerment. Either way, the aim is generally the same – to explore opportunities, to identify, analyse and solve work-related problems and implement solutions. Projects can be chosen by management or when teams work autonomously (as in a quality circle made up of volunteers) they can work on their own identified issues which affect the way they do their work.

People usually enjoy working in teams and find it presents an opportunity for personal and professional development. However, one of the misconceptions which managers sometimes have is that people can automatically work this way. People often need help to overcome the traditional mind-set placed in the way of what is, after all, a different way of working. Hence, effective training will provide a better context and understanding of the processes involved, as well as the skills and the techniques for the team to use. Fundamental to the process is the following:

- generating an environment in which creativity and innovation are encouraged (get away from the fear of making a mistake and being blamed syndrome);
- understanding how this process fits in with management systems (challenging and being comfortable with the notion that managers cannot and do not have to make all the decisions);
- training in the tools and techniques required to contribute effectively in a team.

Problem-solving and creative thinking

Problem-solving is referred to as one of the 'key skills' in the Department for Education and Employment White Paper on the enterprise economy. It has long been acknowledged as one of the essential elements required by employers. Teamed with the skills of communication and working with others, it is a foundation skill enabling creativity to be employed in situations of opportunity or crisis. In the difficult world of higher education today, calls for continuous improvement, effectiveness and efficiency savings can only be met by everyone searching for new and different ways of doing things – sometimes outside the natural constraints of our thinking. Hence the need to develop urgent and enquiring minds able to think creatively and problem-solve effectively.

There is a whole kitbag of techniques and approaches which can help people to develop these skills and for those keen to take some of the principles further there are many books on the power of the brain and how to free it and use it. The most notable series is by Tony Buzan in collaboration with the BBC – the *Use your Head* series which showed how to use the latent power of the mind. Some aspects of these have been taken from the whole and applied separately – hence one often comes across speed-reading classes or memory improvement classes. One of the less well known but very practical techniques is that of mind mapping – a technique for improved note-taking, writing or presentation preparation using a functional approach rather than the linear note-taking traditionally taught and followed at school.

What all of these techniques have in common is the use of the 'whole brain'. Some time ago researchers discovered that we have two sides to the brain, operating different mental areas. In most people the left side deals with logic, words, lists, numbers (the analytical side) whilst the right side deals with imagination, colour, rhythm, awareness and dimension. To be really effective we need to develop and use both sides of the brain to their full potential, but traditionally (and through school) we are taught to think logically. Even our note-taking is encouraged to be set out in lines down the page in sequence. Part of the success of the mind map is to encourage the use of the right brain in organizing ideas and utilizing memory – using links, images, colour and spatial awareness.

Barriers to creativity and problem-solving (and overcoming them)

One of the most powerful barriers to applying these ideas is ourselves. Usually our educational background and upbringing have emphasized the rational and logical approach to dealing with issues in life and at work. So, occasionally at least, it is good to learn to step aside from the norm, and look at things in a different way. There are lots of games and management exercises designed to develop this different approach to things.

Other barriers include the organizations themselves. We've all come across the 'it's always been done that way' syndrome. But what might have been OK ten years ago – and was probably something designed to meet quite adequately the needs then – sometimes needs review and repair or, occasionally, radical overhaul. Very few people are comfortable with challenging traditional ways of thinking (in a meeting with senior management, for example) – hence the fear of looking a fool when offering a different idea can be a powerful disincentive to creativity.

All these are very traditional boundaries or constraints we put on our thinking and it is partly to overcome these barriers that quality team working has proven its value. Remember that some of the most innovative ideas and inventions come from people asking questions such as 'What if. . .?' and 'Why not?'

When a team is trying to think creatively about a problem it will help to remember that:

- there is usually more than one solution (though there may be a 'best fit');
- we are all constrained in our thinking so that it pays to deliberately set this aside to aid our search for innovative solutions;
- most of us are wary of what might be thought of as a foolish idea – so develop and use techniques such as brainstorming to help teams create a sense of trust, openness and fun!

Some problem-solving tools and techniques

Whilst it is not intended to provide detailed instruction on developing and using problem-solving tools and techniques (see references) readers will find it helpful to know what kind of activities and techniques can be used to help the different stages of problem-solving.

Brainstorming

Brainstorming is one of the most effective, simple and frequently used techniques to maximize ideas, involving everyone and breaking down barriers to participation. This can be used for problem selection, analysis and generating solutions. The important thing to remember is not to evaluate ideas when brainstorming – that should come later so that the 'whacky' ideas are accepted – they may prove to be the real winners! Additionally, try structuring the brainstorming process with questions like 'In how many ways can we. . .?' This will give a hook for your ideas; try a warm-up session that everyone can do – it's surprising how many good uses of a paper clip a group can come up with. Allow time for pause and reflection, and try to associate ideas to create new avenues of thought; and of course, it needs enthusiasm, encouragement and a sense of fun which will help cement team identity and team working.

Creative thinking

Creative thinking extends this a little further by encouraging thinking outside the 'normal' constraints of our working environment. As has been said already, some of the most innovative ideas and inventions came from people asking questions such as 'What if. . .?' and 'Why not?'

Pareto analysis

Pareto analysis is a way of analysing the relative value of issues or problems. Simply put, this '80/20' rule can establish, through data analysis, which of the issues, if tackled first, will eliminate most of the problem.

Data collection

Data collection using check sheets, questionnaires and analysing existing data will often be essential in substantiating ideas and solutions and, just as importantly, enabling evaluation later which can prove the effectiveness of the solution.

Fishbone analysis and mind maps

Analysis using fishbone (Ishikawa) diagrams or mind maps (as well as the usual way of presenting information through diagrams, pie charts and histograms) can be a powerful way of representing and organizing ideas and information. The strength of the technique is that it enables the team to look at a problem in several ways, and to demonstrate that it has cons-idered all the options and the effects on other parts of the organization. It also enables the linkages between cause and effect to be shown.

Fishbone diagrams differ from mind maps in that they present a linear linkage. Mind maps are a more organic (whole brain) approach to represent-ing and developing information. Mind maps use a radiating structure to build up a picture of all the information in a clear, focused way, and use colour, shapes, pictures and dimension as an additional stimulus and aid to memory. Described very powerfully by Tony Buzan, it is a very personal technique which many people find particularly powerful.

Fishbone diagrams may look like the one shown in Figure 3.1.

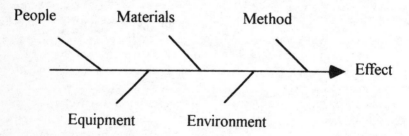

Figure 3.1 *A fishbone diagram (add your own arms and detail)*

Mind maps look like the one shown in Figure 3.2.

SWOT analysis

SWOT analysis is another powerful tool, particularly useful when thinking through plans and strategies; and in this context the likely impact of any solution, hence:

- What are the strengths of this solution (benefits)?;
- What are the weaknesses (what could go wrong)?;

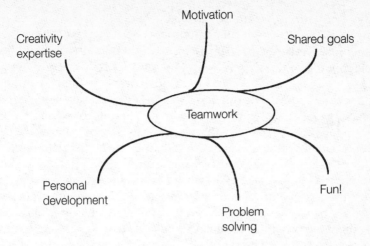

Figure 3.2 *A mind map (add your own colour and pictures!)*

- What opportunities does it give us (for innovation)?;
- What are the threats (dangers) inherent in the solution?

Audit trails and six-word diagrams

Audit trails ask simple but direct questions:

- What are we doing?;
- Why are we doing it that way?;
- How do we know it works?;
- What would we wish to do differently?;
- How could we go about changing it?

This is similar to another method called the six-word diagram which is a simple but none the less effective process asking the six questions, What?, Why?, When?, Where?, Who? and How?

Teams will need to identify which of these techniques will fit their purpose best and part of their training should be to develop a 'kitbag' of tools and techniques which the team can dip into for help at the right time. Being selective as well as creative will be important for progress!

Team development processes and programmes

Many people are familiar with the concept of team development days, often away from the workplace and everyday pressures and contacts in order to reflect on, review and refresh objectives and work practices. There is no doubt that these events represent often essential opportunities to take stock, change and move forward, and they can also be vital in re-establishing communications and understanding within teams.

More dramatic opportunities for both personal and team development through outdoor development programmes and exercises have also become commonplace, adapted as they are from original youth (outward bound) development programmes. Now used widely by industry and the public and private sector, they depend for their success on the opportunity of, together, doing something different from the everyday job, having fun, but also having skilled facilitators to enable participants to reflect on learning points relevant to work and the workplace. (I know that some would probably say abseiling or mountain trekking stretch the definition of fun and the physical nature of the programme is not appropriate for everyone.)

More often people have experienced away days or team development days, either as one-off events designed to help deal with changes and challenges or as routine (perhaps annual) events embraced as a way of doing things, appropriate for senior management and grass-roots and front-line operatives alike. The process again usually involves a facilitator or trainer to encourage and arbitrate discussion, ask the awkward or searching (often 'naïve') question and generally enable people to explore new ideas and challenge the normal and traditional way things may have been done. Hence the use of analytical exercises (SWOT, audit trails) has become commonplace, but is none the less effective to help review and reflection. Sharing information and objectives, building trust and understanding, jointly developing work practices and solving real work problems together all provide a dynamic aid to enhancing job and team performance. So here's your checklist for creative thinking and problem-solving.

Remember the cautionary tales

- there is usually more than one right answer (though there may be one best fit);
- beware the constraints we impose on our thinking – self-imposed barriers including fear of looking a fool;
- develop techniques to encourage team working and creativity in a 'safe' environment free from blame.

Use problem-solving techniques

- brainstorming and maximizing ideas;
- SWOT and audit trails;
- fishbone diagrams and mind maps.

Develop processes for team working and problem-solving and continuous improvement

- quality teams;
- quality circles;
- problem-solving group;
- team development sessions or away days.

Practise and develop other skills

- improve your reading skills and speed;
- improve your memory;
- use mind maps;
- use the left and right brain.

A postscript: an aspirational view of teams and problem-solving

Since all this might seem to make a little too much of bureaucracy and management systems in organizations (almost to the point of sometimes squeezing out the creativity and spontaneity that can quite randomly go on) you can try a dose of different thinking from Tom Peters' book *Crazy Times Call for Crazy Organisations*. I read this again in researching this chapter; it was a refreshing reminder of the different approach that some organizations have taken to prepare themselves for the future and to build on their current success. The book illustrates bold ideas that go beyond total quality management, empowerment and re-engineering the bureaucratic approach that often stifles creativity in employees. Foremost amongst the ideas in Tom Peters' book is the idea of dis-organizing the business to unleash imagination – turning every job into a business, giving everyone the opportunity, support and the means to use independent thinking – 'creating a curious corporation' which enables each and every one to use their knowledge and talents creatively. So here is where problem solving comes in. You probably thought it curious to link a chapter on teams, team working and problem-solving, as not all problems are solved by teams and not all team working is about problem-solving, of course. But what better way for an organization to start to begin to really empower people – and trust them – than by helping them to be really creative and solve problems for the organization by working in a supportive team environment. Not just their usual team but new teams and networks across the organization that break down the traditional barriers, so very often seen in organizations like universities, where jobs are in boxes, people are in departments and may feel constrained by their job descriptions.

So this chapter might be a revolution in itself since it does call for new thinking to build some fun back into work, not just into the training room. It depends on organizations not smothering people. When Peters talks about creating the curious organization he means seriously creating curious people, so that their curiosity is nurtured in a way to develop both their ability to do things that will help the organization and to succeed in the new world order.

I have quite deliberately been selective in listing and adapting some of the 14 ideas given in Tom Peters' book, and have added one or two others to think about.

- Teach curiosity ('Brainstorming is not the answer to creativity but it is an answer'). Invest heavily in using such techniques to solve all problems from purchasing and accounting to quality and marketing.
- Make work fun. Not ha-ha fun, but fun as in enjoyable or refreshing – you know what I mean?
- Change place. Go to work next Thursday and do something different. Make your team building session a night out at a pop concert!
- Establish 'clubs' and networks and bring in outsider support, offbeat educational programmes and measure curiosity. Invite somebody to speak who's doing something extraordinary, contrary to the ordinary corporate style.
- Support general sabbaticals; and insist everyone take vacations; don't let people work overtime by default so that it slips into a routine.
- If there's time for semi-annual performance reviews get employees to write a one page essay instead on the oddest thing I've done this year, the crazy ideas I've had or the five most stupid rules – at least reading performance reviews will be more fun and it might do some good.
- Trust them, train them, then trust them some more (Anita Roddick, Bodyshop).

References

Ackoff, RL (1978) *The Art of Problem Solving*, John Wiley, Chichester.

Buzan, T (1995a) *Use your Head*, BBC Publications, London.

Buzan, T (1995b) *Use your Memory*, BBC Publications, London.

Buzan, T (1995c) *The Mind Map Book*, BBC Publications, London.

CVCP/USDU Task Force 4 (1994) *Approaches Towards the Improvement of Support/Allied Staff Development*, CVCP/USDU, Sheffield.

De Bono, E (1973) *Lateral Thinking*, Harper and Row, New York.

De Bono, E *Mind Mapping* (set of tapes).

De Porter (1994) *Quantum Learning*, Piatkus, London.

Doidge, J and Whitchurch, C (1993) *Total Quality Matters*, Good Practice Guide, AUA, Manchester.

Doidge, J, Bone, D and Hardwick, B (1996) *Quality Teams: Leader Guide and Workbook*, UCoSDA, Sheffield.

Henry, T (1994) *Changing College Culture*, paper presented to NTU Senior Management Conference.

Peters, T (1994) *Crazy Times Call for Crazy Organisations*, Vintage, New York.

Peters, T (1994) *The Tom Peters Seminar*, Vintage, New York.

Woodcock, M (1989) *Team Development Manual*, Gower, Aldershot.

The use of vocational qualifications, standards and competences in the development of allied and support staff

Neil Jones

Introduction

This chapter examines the growth of vocational qualifications (VQs) along with other competence based approaches to the development of allied and support staff. It provides examples of how vocational qualifications are being used at a number of universities and examines some of the factors which promote or constrain the use of standards and competences in staff development.

This chapter also examines two very recent developments in this field (as well as a number of more established competence-based training and development mechanisms) as evidence of a renewed interest in the use of competency-based approaches to performance management and staff development.

The growth of VQs in allied and support staff development

A CVCP survey in 1994 found that 28 per cent of universities were using National Vocational Qualifications (NVQs) in their own staff development and training programmes; moreover, 36 per cent of universities which responded confirmed involvement with the Investors in People initiative. More recent anecdotal evidence suggests that the figure for NVQs is increasing whilst the most recent HEQC *Investors* Network Report now puts the percentage of universities working towards that standard at nearer 50 per cent. Does this begin to suggest a significant shift towards a systematic approach to staff development and, more significantly, that nationally agreed standards of best practice are being embraced by the higher education (HE) sector – or is this too simplistic a response? Clearly, there are a number of factors which impact on the widespread use of VQs, and the growth of other competence-based training and development approaches within the sector:

- There remains a low level of awareness across and within HE institutions about vocational qualifications and their uses in student recruitment, in teaching and learning and consequently in staff training and development.
- There remains a strong cultural tradition which values academic qualifications more highly than vocational ones and pays little attention to the complementary nature of some VQs (eg, linking NVQ levels 4/5 into DMS/MBA programmes). This cultural tradition permeates inevitably through to support staff, many of whom, in considering their own development, still prefer to pursue an academic qualification even where an alternative vocational one may exist.
- The absence of a Higher Education Lead Body (HELB) means that staff within the sector have to pursue qualifications and occupational standards which are inevitably non-sector specific. Whilst it can be argued that the very strength of VQs is their portability and transferability, the need for individuals to fit new skills and behaviours to the HE context means that a valuable opportunity for organizational learning and development – as well as that of the individual – has been lost.
- The absence of an HELB also has an impact upon training and development practitioners who have to become sufficiently familiar with a range of occupational standards and practices and who are often responsible for dealing with the volume of administration and paperwork which accompanies vocational qualifications.
- One of the clearest advantages of using vocational qualifications in training and development is that they allow staff to gain credit for everyday work and the skills they have built up, in some cases over many years. This is particularly appropriate for allied staff for whom, despite the best endeavours of organizations such as the Universities' and Colleges' Staff Development Agency (UCoSDA) and many enthusiastic staff developers, training and development are still not seen as a priority or mainstream issue in a number of universities.
- The freedom, choice and flexibility which underpin vocational qualifications allow staff pursuing them to progress at their own pace, to demonstrate learning in the workplace, and to transfer the skills and

knowledge to a new role or situation; all of these closely mirror the growth of student choice, access, capability, work-based learning and other developments within the HE sector as a whole.

There are already instances of vocational training programmes being used within institutions. Two examples of this are the National Vocational Qualifications (NVQs) and the Management Charter Initiative (MCI).

National Vocational Qualifications (NVQs)

NVQs are now being used as vehicles for training and development in an increasing number of universities. The take up by academic staff is almost exclusively reserved for the Training and Development Lead Body (TDLB) D32, 33 standards. Holders of these awards are able to assess students' workplace learning placements or examine evidence submitted in instances where NVQ units have been built into the curriculum.

The use of NVQs as a feature of allied staff development continues to expand. A recent small-scale survey revealed that their use is greatest with manual workers. Examples include the training of all catering staff at Northumbria, Central Lancashire, Sunderland and Nottingham Trent Universities to a minimum of NVQ level 2, with level 3 being the recognized qualification for catering supervisors. Similar levels of qualification are also becoming the norm for both security and cleaning staff at the above universities.

The use of NVQs is not restricted to manual workers nor is their use confined to the new universities. The Universities of Hull and Leeds both have thriving Business Administration level 3 qualifications in place and there is evidence of increasing innovation in the delivery of such programmes, with one university using video conferencing to provide support for staff in a number of its associate colleges. The rapid developments in the field of information technology (IT) are also being embraced, with a number of universities now offering NVQ level 2 to its users and level 3 to IT specialists in 'user support' teams.

Perhaps the most interesting developments lie in the field of Customer Service NVQs where Leeds, Northumbria, Sunderland and Central Lancashire Universities have established small but enthusiastic groups of candidates – not all of whom occupy traditionally front-line roles – to work towards level 2 and 3 qualifications.

The issue of the assessment and verification of NVQs has been tackled in a variety of ways. Perhaps the favoured approach is to encourage managers to work towards the TDLB assessor standards in order that they may then assess the performance of their own staff in the workplace. This achieves the objectives of keeping ongoing assessment costs low, gaining managers' commitment and ensuring the relevance and transferability of learning. Internal verification may then be carried out by a qualified verifier not involved with the assessment process, or a staff development officer. Elsewhere, the assessment and verification process is managed wholly or partly externally, often with support from the local Training and Enterprise Council (TEC). This is an attractive option where there may be a small number of qualified assessors or verifiers in place, but it nevertheless appears a short-term solution given the inevitable escalation of costs.

However, it is not just in enabling assessment and verification processes that staff developers have a role to play. Perhaps the most challenging and rewarding service that staff developers can provide is one of providing ongoing support to individuals pursuing NVQs. This can take various forms and may include:

- Assistance in portfolio development which can involve helping individuals to choose relevant, sufficient and current evidence for inclusion in the portfolio; or advice on structuring and referencing the portfolio.
- Mentoring of NVQ candidates is very important particularly at times of reduced motivation, where there is little contact with other candidates, or where there may be apathy or even hostility towards the value of NVQs from colleagues and managers.
- The establishment of support groups is a mechanism that staff developers may wish to introduce to help combat some of the difficulties outlined above. The advantages offered by such action learning sets have been well documented and are already a feature of many existing academic courses.
- Keeping candidates' managers informed about NVQs (the low general level of awareness has already been referred to above) and up to date on their staff's progress. The staff developer will need to ensure that a reasonable amount of time is given to staff by managers to collect evidence, attend meetings, etc. Many managers will automatically assume that the work-based nature of these qualifications means that staff can fit the pursuit of the qualification into their daily routine without too much difficulty. This is clearly not the case. In short, staff developers will need to champion the cause of NVQ candidates.

It must be stressed that NVQs do not provide an easy option for personal and professional development. The content, structure and process of such qualifications provide very real challenges to those candidates seeking formal recognition of their competence in the workplace. Furthermore, the challenge of swimming against the cultural tide of academe confronts staff developers and others who are seeking to introduce NVQs in their own institutions.

Management Charter Initiative (MCI)

The MCI standards are based on the four key roles of managing people, managing finance, managing operations and managing information. These are underpinned by a series of personal competences which make up the hidden or soft management skills, eg, 'showing sensitivity to the needs of others', 'identifying and applying concepts'.

Whilst the comment made under the previous heading that NVQs and MCI are well established within many universities is true, the latter has thus far had a minimal impact upon training and development practices in the majority of universities. At first glance MCI seems to be a sound mechanism for developing university managers for the following reasons:

- Many university business schools already have a track record in delivering and assessing MCI programmes for external organizations. Partnerships between staff developers and their academic colleagues could be established to deliver programmes, to support managers through the process and to assess the evidence provided against the Standards.
- The growth of 'managerialism' (Middlehurst, 1994, Miller, 1995) in the late 1980s and early 1990s meant that many staff had some form of management responsibility attached to their jobs. In theory, this group appeared ideal candidates for development and training which would enable them to meet their own and others' expectations of them. The MCI standards are context-free, robust, yet sufficiently flexible to be used in HE manager development.
- Accredited Prior Learning (APL) is an integral feature of the management standards. The opportunity to produce a portfolio demonstrating existing competences backed up by supporting evidence for which credit against the standards may be obtained should be an attractive proposition for some university managers.
- The reflective processes with which managers have to engage to put together a portfolio promotes the 'developmental' approach as opposed to the more typical stand-alone modular management 'training' model. The concept of the reflective practitioner, albeit in an academic context, is one with which academic managers can identify and understand.

Evidence suggests that MCI-based qualifications have made little headway in the sector, nevertheless the MCI standards themselves are being used in various forms. Both Hull and Sunderland Universities use the standards in their first-line and middle management programmes. The University of Northumbria has introduced an MCI-based mentoring programme for senior managers which may lead to a qualification, whilst the University of Glamorgan bases its Framework for Leadership Senior Management Development Programme on the four key roles which make up the MCI standards.

There still remains, however, what one staff developer described as an 'inbuilt prejudice' towards such generic management qualifications by managers in HE who feel they have specialist or professional qualifications that sufficiently equip them to manage staff, resources and their day-to-day operations. Furthermore, the concept of 'management' is still an anathema in old universities in particular where peer approval and decision-making by consensus are still the norm. Even where such ideological difficulties have been overcome, the language used and the fact that the standards do not reflect the culture or vagaries of the sector, both present major obstacles to their gaining widespread acceptance within the sector.

The above are two examples of the use of VQs in staff development. However, there have also been developments in the identification of competences and standards at all levels throughout HE. The following are two examples of such developments which already have important implications for the sector.

ComCon and HERA

The Educational Competences Consortium (ComCon) was established in 1994 by the Universities and Colleges Employers Association (UCEA) with the support of 110 universities and colleges. Its brief was to draw up a series of key roles and associated competences for staff at all levels within the HE sector. The methodology chosen was a combination of traditional job evaluation methods together with behavioural competencies. This approach sought to reconcile both input factors, ie the knowledge, skills, experience and environmental factors, and throughputs which focus on the process by which results are achieved.

The HERA (Higher Education Role Analysis) framework, produced in June 1997, identifies 14 key elements which make up the activities of the 92 roles carried out within the sector. Each of these elements has been given a weighting with 'Teaching and training' at the head of the list and 'Sensory and physical co-ordination' at the bottom. (The full list of weightings is reproduced below.) The value given to 'Teaching and Training' is interesting given that some two-thirds of staff in universities are engaged in support roles.

HERA roles in order of weighting are:

1. Teaching and training
2. Knowledge and experience
3. Initiative and problem-solving
4. Communication
5. Decision-making processes and outcomes
6. Investigation analysis and research
7. Teamwork and motivation

8.   Planning and organizing resources
9.   Service delivery
10. Coaching development and instruction
11. Pastoral care and welfare
12. Work environment
13. Liaison and networking
14. Sensory and physical co-ordination

Although ostensibly a tool to inform and support pay and grading decisions, HERA is also being promoted as a tool for recruitment, appraisal, assessing training needs and planning staff development activities. The rationale is that the recruitment process would attempt to match candidates against a pre-determined job profile; a training plan would then be established to fill the gap between the ideal profile and the actual qualities demonstrated by the postholder. In the longer term HERA would be used to map out a development programme for the individual to take account of changes within the job and his/her own personal and professional development requirements. Clearly, such an approach may be viewed as being too simplistic; of being too task-focused at the expense of the individual and insufficiently flexible to reflect the variety and richness of the knowledge, skills and, more importantly, attitude which underpin the quality of contributions made by employees within the sector.

Nevertheless, the use of HERA does offer a genuine attempt to promote a systematic approach to training and developing staff. For too long, training and development practitioners within the sector have questioned the validity and appropriateness of largely competence-based models in favour of a more pragmatic approach. The result is that whilst HERA does have weaknesses, staff developers, in particular those dealing with support staff and those housed within personnel departments, may come under pressure to adopt such a model to inform their own training and development practices.

UCoSDA Occupational and Functional Mapping Exercise

In May 1997, UCoSDA produced the final report of a year-long project which sought to identify occupations, functions and existing qualification pathways in higher education. In the longer term it was hoped that the exercise would help to identify gaps in existing staff development provision and ultimately provide a framework for training and development which met the disparate and diverse needs of all employees within the sector.

In the foreword to the report UCoSDA stated that the purpose of the mapping exercise was 'firmly developmental' and that it had 'no association with job evaluation'. This was an explicit attempt to distance the project

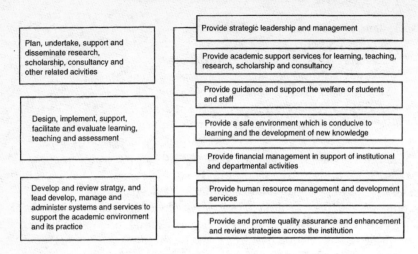

Figure 4.1 *UCoSDA functional frame of the HE sector: key areas of activity with extracts from associated units (March 1997)*

from the work carried out in support of ComCon (see above) around the same time. Despite logistical and initial methodological concerns a functional frame of the HE sector (produced in part as Figure 4.1) was produced.

In producing the report, UCoSDA notes that the mapping project was a discrete exercise and merely suggests a series of options for moving forward; these vary from halting the process following dissemination of the report to the development of a complete set of standards which may eventually lead to the implementation of NVQ levels 1–5 in higher education.

At present the practical value of the standards to training and development practitioners within the sector is open to question. The report itself acknowledges the already wide-ranging links between HE institutions and lead bodies. It is likely that the standards developed by the lead bodies will, for the most part, continue to inform the staff development practices and vocational qualifications provision for staff within the sector. However, the report does contribute greatly to the completion of a national occupational framework to Level 5 and, whilst using the N/SVQ approach of functional analysis, the standards do appear to have retained the richness, diversity and complexity of the professional activities carried out in higher education.

Investors in People (IIP)

Whilst it may initially appear unusual to include Investors in People when examining the development of vocational qualifications, there are a number of parallels between Investors and other competence-based approaches to training and development.

- It is a national standard (industry-wide but not sector-specific) which could be defined as an NVQ for the organization. The standard is made up of four key principles (or units of competence in NVQ terms) which break down into 23 indicators (elements). Further assessment guidance (performance criteria and range statements) is available to support organizations working towards Investors status.
- Evidence that an organization submits in support of its submission to become an Investor in People is usually found in the form of a portfolio and the assessment against the standard primarily takes place in the workplace.
- Time scales are flexible and organizations are free to work towards achievement of the standard at their own pace and in a manner appropriate to the organization. Indeed, some organizations have achieved Investors by covert means by putting systems and processes in place and only declaring to employees at a later stage that the award was formally being sought; this to avoid the danger of fad or initiative overload!
- An Investors in People organization must demonstrate ongoing competence and must be re-assessed every three years to ensure continuing compliance with the standard.

Whilst there have been concerns that Investors in People does not fit the HE culture; that the language is too business orientated (attempts continue to translate the standard into 'HE speak'); that it focuses solely on loyalty to the organization and not to the academic discipline or profession, some 70 universities and colleges are currently working towards the standard. For allied and support staff this is highly encouraging as achievement of Investors in People status requires a demonstrable commitment to the development of all staff, a commitment still lacking in a number of UK universities.

The challenge ahead

The absence of adequate resources for allied staff development, in contrast to their academic colleagues, has meant that allied staff, and allied staff developers in particular, have become more opportunistic, focused and systematic in seeking out training and development opportunities. The challenge now for allied staff developers is to recognize where vocational qualifications, national standards and competence-based training can offer an opportunity for realistic, relevant and worthwhile development to individuals and their institutions, and to embrace such opportunities wholeheartedly. Where external standards do not exist or are deemed inappropriate – and a decision on their appropriateness should not be taken lightly – alternative methods of accreditation should be explored, eg institutions' Credit Accumulation Transfer (CAT) schemes.

It must be stressed that VQs in themselves are not training programmes and their introduction will require staff developers to move away from the cycle of short course delivery (which often reflects a personal expertise rather than an institutional need) and to develop new ways of working and thinking. In particular this will require staff developers to work in areas which are unfamiliar to them or where they do not have 'expert power'. The move to vocationalism will require them to acknowledge and embrace best practice from outside the sector (which does not necessarily mean the wholesale importation of such practice) and to develop links with local TECs.

This is a challenge which will require allied staff developers to display the innovation, creativity, tenacity and verve which has characterized their work over the last ten years, and which has led to the development of support staff as being a key feature of most universities' training and development practice.

References

Middlehurst, R (1994) *Leading Academics*, SRHE/Open University Press, Buckingham.

Miller, HDR (1995) *The Management of Change in Universities*, SRHE/Open University Press, Buckingham.

UCoSDA (1997) *Occupational and Functional Mapping of the HE Sector in Great Britain*, UCoSDA, Sheffield.

HEQC (1995) *Vocational Qualifications and Standards in Focus*, HEQC, London.

HEQC (1995) *Investors in People in Higher Education Progress Report*, UCoSDA/HEQC, Sheffield.

——5——

To accredit, or not to accredit?

Pat King

Development of university staff

Ten years ago in the depths of the recession, universities were being urged to consider the development of their staff:

> There are few matters of greater importance to the future of the university than the quality, dedication, motivation and productivity of . . . staff. Insofar as these are endangered by current trends, they deserve the closest attention and concern from the authorities of each system.
>
> (Taylor, 1987)

Staff development in its widest sense is a significant tool in helping people to manage change. Training can teach individuals new skills, or improve and update their existing skills. Small teams can be encouraged to assess their effectiveness and re-focus their energies. Larger units can be facilitated to develop their perspectives in order to meet the new challenges. Wise organizations use this tool strategically to address the wider issues and to ensure a smoother transition period for all their staff.

Traditionally, academic staff development has concentrated predominantly on the individual updating of subject specialisms. Many institutions with a strong teaching focus set up small units to look at educational development issues, and staff development for lecturers became part of the remit for these units. Support staff development, where it existed, was traditionally the responsibility of a registrar or a senior academic.

In 1988 the Fender Report concluded that 'Despite recent effort in universities to improve the training and staff development of non-academic staff the total effort is small compared with that in successful companies' and recommended that universities 'should make a major new investment in staff development and training'. This resulted in a number of universities appointing a staff development officer, usually reporting through the personnel department, to take on the brief for support staff.

Today, the abundance and pace of change in HE, and particularly the introduction of accountability, have prompted institutions to focus their attention more on staff development than at any other time in their history. The Universities' and Colleges' Staff Development Agency's (UCoSDA) Task Force 4 concluded:

> Never before in higher education has the importance of and the need for well trained and developed support/allied staff been as vital as it is today. With the emphasis on quality, through assessment and audit, featuring ever more prominently, the roles and responsibilities of support/allied staff have taken on a greater significance.
>
> (UCoSDA, 1994)

Fundamental changes inevitably affect the way people work. Expedience means that the traditional roles and practices of different categories of staff have come under closer scrutiny, and the edges between them are increasingly blurred. Which begs the question: how can we ensure that staff are competent to perform these multi-faceted roles?

Key issues for support staff development

Support staff often welcome staff development, particularly when leading to a qualification, because they see it as a means of improving their status within their institution, and their prospects beyond it. Institutions also have reasons for introducing accredited staff development. Those pursuing Investors in People find it relevant to satisfy both the overall ethos of the standard, as well as several of the indicators. It can also provide a useful resource for the appraisal process.

However, several key issues dominate any attempt to develop accredited staff development for support staff. First, the custom of labelling all non-teaching staff under a heading such as support, as if it accurately represented a single homogeneous group. These staff practise a wide range of professions and skills, and include: librarians, technicians, administrators, caterers, secretaries, those responsible for cleaning and maintaining buildings, public relations, human resources, legal and constitutional issues, health and safety, student and staff interests and records, finance, computing, student recruitment and admissions, sports, welfare and accommodation. They might be employed under the same contract, but their work is so diverse that no single form of staff development could begin to cover all areas. Moreover, terms other than support are used in many universities, for example, allied, ancillary, non-teaching, academic-related, making it difficult to put an accurate label on the publicity for staff development activities.

Second, even within certain groups, there is no agreement about what the group name implies. For example, the term administrator implies a senior function closely linked to academia in pre-1992 universities, whereas the post-1992 universities would describe nearly all office-based staff as administrators; technicians are usually understood to be those who support academic staff in the teaching and learning process, yet some institutions interpret this term more broadly to include those working in computing and in maintenance areas. With so little agreement about status and terminology, staff development events could have difficulty in reaching the right audience.

Third, while many support staff might devote their entire careers to HE, many more will both come from, and return to, other sectors, both private and public. An effective staff development programme needs both to acknowledge the skills and experience brought to the sector by those who have worked outside it, and at the same time to channel that experience into the context of higher education. For example, an accountant with several years' experience in the private sector would need to continue developing financial management skills, as well as learning about the national and local forces which control and constrain university income and expenditure.

Fourth, because of the mobility of support staff, they are likely to be most attracted to undertake qualifications that are nationally recognized, and therefore portable, such as those awarded by the various professional bodies and National Vocational Qualifications (NVQs). Any accredited staff development which limits itself solely to higher education could be perceived as having limited value to those who envisage moving out of HE later in their careers.

Finally, professional and vocational qualifications improve and validate the specialism being pursued to a standard that is recognized in all sectors of the workforce, including HE. What they lack, however, is any contextualization within HE. Even NVQs which are demonstrated by work carried out in HE, do not require that staff understand the wider national factors within which their institution, and their own departments, have to function.

Staff development groups in HE

During the past few years, many lively networks of staff developers have grown up in geographical areas to discuss, develop and deliver local events. In addition, several national organizations have formed, or been set up, with a focus on staff development in HE. They put on a range of activities, produce a variety of publications, disseminate information, and attempt to influence HE policy on behalf of their membership.

Association of University Administrators (AUA)

The AUA plays an active role in developing the professional skills of managers and administrators at all levels throughout HE. It offers a programme of seminars and workshops throughout the year and provides readers of its electronic bulletin and newsletter with up-to-date information on professional development and HE issues. Its refereed journal is a forum for research and debate on policy issues.

The annual AUA Conference provides participants with the opportunity to tailor-make their own training programme from over 250 working and networking sessions and lectures from key decision-makers in HE. It is also an opportunity for individuals to gain experience in presenting sessions in their own area of expertise. The AUA has a well developed information exchange and network of reciprocal arrangements with organizations abroad. This enables a global exchange of best practice in HE management and the development of international networks.

Although it is not an accrediting body, a principal objective of the AUA is to actively support the professional development activities of those committed to developing a career in HE. In this connection, it was represented by Keith Jones on the SCAMAD panel which has developed a modular Masters programme, and by Jeannette Collins on the SEDA Committee which has devised an accredited Professional Development Programme in HE.

Universities' and Colleges' Staff Development Agency (UCoSDA)

UCoSDA was established in 1989 as part of the Committee of Vice-Chancellors and Principals (CVCP) as the central organization to support higher educational institutions (HEIs) in their provision of training and development for all groups of their employees. UCoSDA's overarching aim is to promote strategically planned, continuing, relevant and coherent staff development for all staff in HE and it therefore is involved in training and development sector-wide.

UCoSDA's key staff development and training services include the provision of an advisory and help line service; facilitation of expert consortia, task forces, project teams and networks, etc; consultancy and training; regular mailings to all HEIs; a free loan resources service; a range of tailored publications; and the organization of national and regional conferences, courses, seminars and workshops on topical themes in staff development. It has as one of its objectives the development of accreditation schemes, as appropriate to all staff groups, linking with accreditation bodies and building on work already undertaken. For example, currently in development is a Master's programme for HE administrators and managers which will be validated by centres across the UK. The programme will be modular in structure and assessments, work-based modules, dissertation and project modules, etc and the participants will have the option of working towards certificate, diploma or Master's level qualifications.

UCoSDA will continue its support of management, career and continuing professional development for all HE employees and in terms of accreditation will build on its work in respect of higher educational qualifications, eg, in academic practice and teaching and learning; quality assessment work with the funding councils; and vocational qualifications, where appropriate, for a range of functions and staff groups.

Staff and Educational Development Association (SEDA)

SEDA is a collaborative organization of HE practitioners concerned with the encouragement of innovation and good practice in staff and educational development. It puts on national conferences and other events, publishes a wide range of books and papers, co-ordinates a number of regional and specialist networks and collaborates with many others, and has developed three accreditation schemes: for teachers, for staff and educational developers in HE, and for Professional Development in HE.

SEDA accreditation of Professional Development in Higher Education (PDHE)

Four years ago a group of staff and educational developers set out to develop a scheme which had, at its heart, the desirability of building bridges between different categories of staff by encouraging collaboration in their staff development. This ethos was later expressed by Lewis Elton as follows: 'because of the interlocking responsibilities of different staff, the development of different categories of staff should not be kept organizationally separate from each other' (1995). A second premise was that a single, cohesive framework for staff development applicable to all staff would enable an institution to take a strategic approach in managing the changing nature of its work. As a result, a SEDA committee was formed with representatives from 17 organizations comprising HE institutions, the AUA and UCoSDA. The committee developed the scheme, seeking feedback and contributions from large numbers in the sector. In December 1996, the scheme to accredit Professional Development in Higher Education was formally launched.

The PDHE is a framework suitable for all categories of HE staff, within which there is sufficient flexibility for institutions to design or adapt staff development programmes appropriate to their own needs, culture and setting. In order to gain SEDA recognition of their programmes, institutions must ensure that candidates demonstrate six objectives underpinned by seven values, as follows:

Underpinning values

1. The experience of students – a significant focus for all staff.
2. The learning experience of staff.

3. Commitment to higher education.
4. The contribution of all staff in pursuing high quality.
5. Continued reflection and improvement on working practice in HE.
6. Team working.
7. Practising equal opportunities.

Objectives to be demonstrated

1. Interpersonal skills which enable effective communication with staff, students and outside agencies, where appropriate, using oral, written and other relevant techniques.
2. The capability for prioritizing and organizing their workload, initiating and responding to new ideas and requests, and reorganizing work in the light of new requirements.
3. An understanding of their role within their own institution and the wider context of HE.
4. Personal and professional coping strategies within the constraints and opportunities of their institutional setting.
5. Reflection on their own personal and professional needs, and in particular their continuing professional development.
6. The ability to use their specialist knowledge and skills appropriately in the HE context.

In addition, candidates must be involved in both formal learning (such as professional, vocational, academic or staff development courses) and experiential learning (through work). These two related elements are recorded and reflected on by candidates.

A key element of the PDHE scheme is that programmes must demonstrate that they build bridges between different categories of staff. Aside from this, institutions have flexibility to decide the type and extent of staff development they wish to have recognized by SEDA. Following formal recognition of their institution's programme, successful candidates are awarded a SEDA certificate.

Institutions are attracted to the scheme for a range of reasons, some of which are:

- the focus on strategic staff development;
- to gain national recognition of an existing programme;
- to provide support for appraisal;
- to support their pursuit of Investors in People;
- to develop programmes in collaboration with colleagues in the sector, against a national benchmark;
- to share ideas for developing particular groups of staff.

As a result, institutions have taken a wide variety of approaches to the scheme, such as:

- the adaptation of an existing taught modular course in order to gain national recognition of a diploma programme for academic and support managers (see Appendix A);
- the development of a workbook for all staff which prompts candidates to investigate the wider context within which they work;
- revamping the central workshop programme requiring external trainers to anchor their courses to PDHE values and objectives, and setting up a resources room for staff containing written, audio and compact disc interactive materials;
- extended induction based on a series of workshops and assignments building into a reflective portfolio, with each candidate supported by a sponsor;
- a link between teacher accreditation and the PDHE aimed at staff with responsibilities both inside and outside the classroom;
- the adaptation of a programme for technicians to follow an NVQ-type model, supported by peer groups and an external portfolio building adviser;
- the amalgamation of formal sessions based on a core programme of generic skills and independent learning supported by a mentoring scheme and portfolio development;
- the development of a continuing professional development (CPD) framework for all staff, accredited by SEDA.

Local initiatives

Over the past decade, there has been a proliferation in the number and range of initiatives to train and develop support staff, and a range of excellent examples is appended to UCoSDA's Task Force Four publication. Often the impetus has come from staff developers' concern that the development needs of large numbers of these staff were being overlooked. This impetus has been reinforced by the advent of quality audit and quality assessment, and the dawning realization by senior managers that: 'Since support/allied staff make a vital contribution to the overall student experience, what they do and how they do it, will inevitably be assessed as part of this process' (UCoSDA, 1994).

Most initiatives have been either devised by staff developers or adapted by them from activities that have succeeded elsewhere, often in the private sector. Many are aimed at improving the skills of particular categories of staff for whom little or no provision was otherwise available (see Staffordshire University's cleaner training, UCoSDA, 1994, Appendix 1), and for those with particular types of responsibility, such as supervisors and managers (see Leeds Metropolitan's Gateway Programme, UCoSDA, 1994, Appendix 3), as well as the more general approach (such as the University of Surrey's staff exchange scheme). Many have come about as a result of the increasing legislation connected with health and safety, whether from Britain or the European Community.

With the exception of the latter, which are mandatory, most are local in nature, being devised by and for the staff in one institution. Given the collaborative nature of staff developers in HE, there is a considerable willingness to share ideas, successes and failures with each other, whether via national conferences, regional networks and written materials, in order to improve the services each can offer in their own institutions. Examples of such collaboration can be found in various regional programmes, such as the seminars for technicians organized by Ken Bromfield of King's College London whereby a network of university technicians working in the London region put on low-cost technician training (UCoSDA, 1994, Appendix 9), the management and leadership programme for senior support staff run jointly by Heriot-Watt, Dundee, Stirling and St Andrews (UCoSDA, 1994, Appendix 6), specialist training events for administrators put on by the Southern Universities Administrative Training Committee, and Central Lancashire's Postgraduate Diploma in Education Administration and Management which is available to its own support staff, as well as those in partner colleges and institutions in the North West.

Many universities have devised their own formal staff development policy that, in greater or lesser detail, sets out the value, nature and purpose of staff development. Even institutions without a written policy nevertheless operate staff development within an overall framework which embraces many of the themes to be found in a formal policy, such as:

- institutional responsibility for staff development;
- individual responsibility for lifelong learning;
- the equitable distribution of funds, time and other resources;
- staff development linked to strategic aims, while including personal development;
- the role of staff development in improving the motivation and morale of staff.

Local initiatives have tended to concentrate on personal and vocational skills development. Significantly, most are unaccredited, except where an institution decides to issue its own local certification, and many are designed in isolation from the teaching and learning functions of the university.

These last two factors play a key role in support staff development, for while any kind of training is welcome in this formerly arid area, staff increasingly seek some kind of recognition for their staff development activities, particularly something portable across and beyond the sector. Additionally, staff developers working with these groups are increasingly aware that training skills in isolation from the core activities of the institution (teaching, learning, and research) can fail to underpin the training within a context of HE.

Other support staff, such as librarians, accounting and personnel special-ists, have also received relatively little attention from their institutions. However, those who have gained membership of professional associations often look for opportunities for training and for updating qualifications from their professional bodies.

As a result of all this activity, there has been a significant raising of consciousness among support staff regarding the possibilities of staff development, so that increasingly the impetus is coming from staff themselves. This has emerged as a desire not just for a wide range of training opportunities, but also for some sort of certificate in recognition of their efforts, particularly one that has national currency.

National Vocational Qualifications

An increasing number of institutions are introducing NVQs, often in collaboration with their local further education college. The main attractions for staff lie in the portability of NVQs across all sectors of the workforce, the availability of a national qualification in areas where little else exists (eg for experienced secretaries), and the perceived improved employability of NVQ qualified people. Staff gaining an NVQ often report that the two most valuable outcomes have been, first, the experience has made them reflect more closely on what they do and why they do it in that particular way, and second, an improvement in their confidence. In these respects, those who achieve NVQs (and who survive the inevitable bureaucratic paper-chase) certainly perceive their efforts as developmental.

In-house accreditation

An alternative approach is the certification of in-house staff development courses. Some institutions award certificates of attendance, but more highly prized are the certificates awarded as a result of successfully achieving the required outcomes of the course, as these indicate a certain amount of improvement in the candidate's abilities. While an invaluable public recognition that a particular course is taken seriously in a particular HE institution, such certificates inevitably lack the portability of a national qualification. One solution is to credit-rate the course, providing a structure for candidates to progress to other level courses (see Nottingham Trent's Certificate in Personal and Professional Development, UCoSDA, 1994, Appendix 4).

Additionally, many HE staff register as students on courses taught at their own institutions. In the past, universities have been fairly generous in subsidizing the cost (in full or in part) for their own staff. However, hard times mean that this generosity is dwindling. Some HE staff, for various reasons, will be subsidized to register for courses taught at other institutions.

Whether staff wish to study in their own institution or elsewhere, three difficulties face them:

1. most HE courses require considerable time and commitment from the individual, leading to an uneasy juggling act between study and heavy workloads;
2. many HE courses require candidates to attend day-time lectures and tutorials, and the candidates' absence from work places a burden on the managers and colleagues who must provide cover;
3. the entry requirements for HE courses can be prohibitive for large numbers of support staff.

Looking ahead

While it is always dangerous to try to predict the future, two general trends in staff development have been detected by a wide range of practitioners, and succinctly summed up by David Boud (1995):

1. 'increasingly there will be a focus on learning occurring in natural work-groupings, whether these be departments, research teams or offices';
2. 'developing reflective practice within the context of the normal working environment will increasingly become central to any staff development activity.'

A steady and discernible movement towards team working is beginning to erode the barriers between categories of staff. At the same time, budget constraints and heavy workloads make it increasingly difficult to send numbers of staff to external, or even internal, events. As a result, both staff development for teams comprising different categories of staff, and accredited work-based learning, become highly attractive.

However, these approaches do require appropriate structural support. In the first case, it makes little sense for staff developers to promote cross-category teamwork if they themselves operate a demarcation of responsibilities, often endorsed by their institutions, for the development of academic and support staff. In the second case, staff pursuing work-based learning have to be well organized and motivated. They need their institution to allocate time for learning and reflection in the same way that it allocates time to off-site learning, and to formalize this time by means of a learning agreement. They may also need training to help them assemble a portfolio, with alternative approaches for those not comfortable with writing.

Many institutions are introducing continuing professional development, encouraging staff to plan their careers, to record the full range of activities they are engaged in, to identify their staff development requirements, and to gain or upgrade their qualifications. The beauty of Continuing

Professional Development (CPD) is that it formally acknowledges the wide range of unaccredited staff development activities that people are involved in, such as work-shadowing, staff exchanges within and beyond the institution, participation in conferences and seminars, appropriate reading, computer-based information gathering, and engagement in staff networks.

Several professional bodies and private training organizations produce CPD packages; alternatively, HE institutions may find it more appropriate to develop their own. (For example, Matt Levi, of the University of Exeter, is working on a model involving mandatory and optional elements, agreed in consultation with line management and a D32/33 qualified assessor, with a personal development plan closely tied in to induction, probation and the SEDA PDHE qualification.)

Systems for gaining credits are increasingly available throughout the sector, providing the means for busy staff to gain qualifications at their own pace. A number of projects have been funded by the Department for Education and Employment to encourage the wider use of Credit Accumulation Transfer (CAT). Some HE institutions use the Accreditation of Prior Experiential Learning (APEL) in order to broaden access to academic qualifications, while others credit Foundation level courses for the same purpose. Others focus on using credit from prior learning to facilitate entry with advanced standing. There are also schemes being developed to award credit for CPD.

While acknowledging the significant benefits of unaccredited staff development, economic reality has led to an increasing demand for accreditation based on the perception that those with qualifications have the edge, in the job market, over those without. How long this trend continues depends on whether a saturation point emerges over time.

What seems certain in this uncertain world is that it is no longer safe for anyone in the workforce to rely on 'the measles approach to learning: have it young and you should not have it for the rest of your life' (John Berkeley, Rover Group, THES). In some respects, a qualification is like a passport: it can open doors for the bearer, but is not much use if it is out of date. The ethos of higher education is to encourage the pursuit of lifelong learning. Why not apply this ethos to our essential staff?

Appendix A

The first programme to be recognized by SEDA under the new Professional Development in Higher Education scheme was the Professional Development Diploma in General Management Skills developed by staff development officers at the University of Hull. The SEDA programme was formed by revising a series of existing workshops and by developing assessment methods which mapped onto SEDA objectives and values.

The staff development office at the University of Hull is committed to working towards providing a wide range of accredited and recognized programmes. Perceived benefits to the University of Hull are that:

- institutional objectives are achieved by equipping staff with the skills, knowledge and abilities necessary to fulfil these goals;
- formal recognition of development activities increases candidates' motivation to undertake the programme;
- it increases the profile and professionalism of staff development.

The development of the General Management Skills programme and its subsequent recognition by SEDA also ensure that university colleagues who successfully gain this Award have their development formally acknowledged by the achievement of a nationally recognized qualification. Due to the formal qualification attached to this programme of study, colleagues who participate believe that they will enhance their career development opportunities both within (and beyond) their current university context.

The programme, which is open to all categories of staff who manage people, operations, information or finance, consists of 20 workshops in five modules which explore the skills of effective management within a higher education context. The five modules are:

- Personal Skills
- Process Skills
- People Skills
- Product Skills
- Policy Skills

Participants are given activities to undertake prior to each workshop and these act as a focal point during the workshop for discussion, further exercises, reflection on practical experience and some contextual input on relevant theory. The workshops are a catalyst for development and participants enhance their personal learning based on the SEDA values and objectives through the assessment process. The learning design of the programme utilizes the Learning Cycle developed by Honey and Mumford and emphasizes the need for reflection and evaluation as a key ingredient in developing managerial skills.

Assessment is based on the production of three assignments (focusing on the functions of HE institutions, health and safety at work and equal opportunities) and a Learning Portfolio. All the assessed work is constructed to provide the opportunity for linking experience, reflection, action planning and improvement of practice supported by theoretical knowledge and understanding.

A major part of the assessment is the Learning Portfolio. This work is based on the production of a personal development plan which details the journey that the candidate will make between their current and desired level of skills, knowledge and abilities in the field of management. The personal development plan is based on the SEDA values and objectives and is the foundation for the Learning Portfolio which demonstrates in both academic and practical terms the candidate's progress toward their desired development goals.

Members of the staff development office act as personal supervisors to the candidates. Peer support groups of three or four people are also established. This group provides a forum for sharing ideas, concerns and mutual support relating to progress on the programme. Additionally, the peer support group also provides feedback to each other on certain skill-based activities such as, for example, presentations and selection interviewing.

Along with SEDA recognition, the programme is also accredited through the University of Hull as a Professional Development Diploma which is credit rated at 120 Master level points.

References

Berkeley, J *Times Higher Education Supplement*, 7 March 1997.

Boud, D (1995) 'Meeting the challenges', in A. Brew (ed.), *Directions in Staff Development*, SRHE and OU Press, Buckingham.

Elton, L (1995) 'An institutional framework', in A. Brew (ed.), *Directions in Staff Development*, SRHE and OU Press, Buckingham.

Fender, B (1988) *Investing in People*, CVCP, London.

Taylor W (1987) *Universities under Scrutiny*, OECD, Paris.

UCoSDA (1994) *Approaches towards the Improvement of Support/Allied Staff Development*, Task Force Four, UCoSDA, Sheffield.

——6——

The impact of new technology and implications for support and allied staff training

Jenny Wilkinson

Twenty years ago forward-looking departments purchased electronic type-writers and prided themselves on obtaining the latest in office technology. Ten years ago the same departments were looking to the future and considering the purchase of a computer. Now every clerical member of a department expects that they will have a computer on their desk, on which they can not only produce letters and memos, but can, if necessary, link to the World Wide Web and surf the Internet. The pace and degree of change are outstanding and it is a credit to the flexibility and willingness of staff that individuals have continued to develop their skills in line with demands.

This chapter examines the importance of information technology (IT) within the university environment and will emphasize the need for appropriate and effective training of allied and support staff. Common pitfalls in IT training will be identified as well as the key steps required for getting it right.

The importance of information technology and IT training

It would be impossible to ignore the dramatic increase in the use of computers in university departments over the last five years. Almost all clerical jobs now rely on a computer to produce written documentation, prepare statistics, record student details and a million other tasks besides. The impact of computers on technical jobs can be equally marked and there is no doubt that technical staff feel an increasing requirement to become computer literate.

The financial difficulties of the university sector are well rehearsed and it is clear that to some extent information technology is central to creating some of the efficiency gains required to help higher education through its current funding difficulties. There are doubtless many administrative procedures which could be improved through the increased use of computers. Information technology is challenging traditional methods of communication: many institutions now make their prospectus available on the Web and distance learners are encouraged to apply for details of courses via the Internet. How long will it be before the majority of students are approaching universities in this way and what impact will that have upon current admissions procedures? In the broader field of delivering education, developments in the use of computers for teaching are altering pupil or student learning experiences from primary school onwards. It is essential that universities harness these opportunities, plan for them and train staff in the efficient operation and use of computing resources.

Despite the obvious importance of information technology, universities continue to underestimate the training requirements of allied staff. There is still an incessant demand for computer training and although I have no evidence to support this, other than personal experience, I would venture to suggest that by far the largest area of training requests arising from appraisal is for IT courses. It would seem that the more you offer people, the more they want, and whatever you offer it is never enough.

Pitfalls of IT training

Why are people still demanding training and feeling under-supported with regard to IT? It would be easy to claim that the pace of change outstrips the speed at which training can be developed and delivered. I believe, however, that there are a number of common pitfalls surrounding the delivery of IT training, largely related to staff expectations and assumptions made by university administrators or managers, which contribute to the problem.

'Surely they will just pick it up – I did'

There appears to be a common theory that people can learn how to use a computer through some sort of mysterious process of osmosis. There is an assumption, by some managers, that if you sit a person in front of a computer they will instinctively learn how to use it without any support or training, rather like placing someone in the middle of France and expecting them to learn French. Clearly, necessity will eventually lead to some level of understanding, but this method is hardly effective and will probably lead to little more than a basic level of skill being acquired. Despite the introduction of staff training and developments units in many institutions and the increased emphasis on training, many staff are still presented with a computer, a pile of manuals (if they are lucky) and expected to make the most of it. An academic member of the department will probably have installed the software and provided instruction as to what they want produced, then left that person to their own devices.

'Well, you've been on the training course – you must be an expert!'

Expectations of staff who have been on training courses are often unreasonably high, both from others and from the person themselves. Staff who have recently received training often feel under pressure to perform to speed immediately whereas the reality is that it would probably be quicker to chisel documents in stone. They also feel that they should be experts, whereas in fact they are still inexperienced learners. This problem is heightened on their return to their department, especially if they are the only person to have been trained, as they now assume guru status.

'We've got the best computers in the department – that will make work easier'

It is understandable that institutions will be keen to purchase the best equipment available and want to subscribe to the latest release of a piece of software; however, expenditure on training is not commensurate with expenditure on equipment. Consequently many departments are in the position of owning modern, sophisticated equipment and not being able to achieve the most effective results with it. This is akin to buying a jumbo jet and overlooking the need for a trained pilot with a current pilot's licence. Investment in training is just as important as expenditure on equipment when it comes to improving the productivity and effectiveness of an office or department, and yet is rarely budgeted for.

'I went on a course, but I forgot it all'

This is such a common complaint, and the problem lies not with the course but with the expectation of the person who attended it. Many people think that going on a training course is all they need to do to become proficient in the use of a piece of software. Very few people would use the same technique for their driving test and expect to pass after just a couple of lessons. The need to practise computer skills with a realistic piece of work is vitally important and it is this element which is usually neglected when people are learning. Departments and managers need to encourage staff to practise, make it safe for them to spend time 'playing' with and therefore learning about IT.

'Nellie told Tom, Tom told me!'

Cascade training has its place. However, if it is to be used to share skills in a department it needs to be monitored very closely by someone who has a good understanding of the software in question. In principle the idea is sound; send one of the department on a training course and ask them to teach the others on their return. At its best this can work very well and be an effective way of disseminating information throughout an office. At its worst it can become as inefficient as Chinese whispers. Much of the success relies on the source person being, first of all, able to learn and absorb the initial training and, second, able to pass that knowledge on to other members of staff. On the whole, this is a fairly unstable method of training and, unless carefully monitored and planned for, is probably best avoided.

'We are brilliant at training the students in IT, why don't we just get the secretaries and technicians to sit in on the student classes?'

Whilst the efficiency in terms of time and training resources of this approach is obvious, the long-term effectiveness for staff is questionable. Staff and students have very different learning styles and expectations of learning. Students are unlikely to be intimidated by the possibility of 'playing' and practising with a piece of software since, after all, learning is what they are at university to do. Staff, on the other hand, are at university to work, and they feel uncomfortable when they are not doing something immediately constructive or productive. They would not, therefore, feel the same freedom to try things out. Staff need courses tailored to their needs where they can very quickly learn how to use the computer to support their work. Since their work is different from that of a student it is hardly appropriate to expect them to learn alongside a student. After all, staff are not students and should not be treated in the same way as students. Staff should be entitled to training which is geared to their needs and attended by staff only. What messages are we sending to our staff if we cannot supply them with dedicated training to help them perform their work to the best of their ability?

Key steps to getting IT training right

As with all training, developing the computing skills of adults requires thought and planning. In particular, the following steps should always be considered when providing computer training:

Sensitivity

It goes without saying that trainers need to be sensitive to the needs of their client group, and this is especially important in relation to IT training.

Many people feel extremely vulnerable when on the receiving end of IT training – whether it is being delivered as a class-based taught course or on a one-to-one basis. The trainer has to be aware, at all times, of the impact that the introduction of a computer into someone's work area can have, particularly if this is the first time they have been expected to use one. Imagine being a technician who has worked in a department's store for years. One day you are presented with a computer and told that it is now departmental policy for the stores records to be computerized. Suddenly you find that you cannot do your job anymore, not because you don't understand the job, but because you don't know how to get the computer to perform the tasks required. It wouldn't be surprising if you felt intimidated and resentful. Another example that I witnessed was that of an experienced and highly efficient secretary who, on the introduction of computers into her office, remarked that computers were de-skilling. Far from being impressed by the spell-checking facility provided by the word processor, she instead felt stripped of her skills and devalued, as the ability to spell had been a secretarial quality in which she took great pride.

Good IT trainers have to take account of these considerations and design their courses with these issues in mind. As with most training, results are more effective if the trainer takes account of the trainees' concerns and helps them to overcome them. This can usually be done by encouraging people to identify areas, for themselves, where the computer can enhance their work. When IT is seen as an imposition from above, the reluctance to learn about it is very strong. In many ways, courses need to be designed not only to teach the required skill, but to encourage acceptance of the new office tool and way of working.

Timing

Correct timing of an IT course is imperative. If a person attends a course before they are ready to practically apply their new skills there is a strong chance that their time will be wasted, as will the trainer's. A further knock-on effect is that that person will then avoid any further training on that particular piece of software or IT skill as they will feel that they had their chance and they lost it.

Staff should be encouraged to attend courses when they need them and not before. There is a tendency for staff to enthusiastically anticipate their needs and go along to courses before they are using a piece of software. Effective transfer of new learned skills to the workplace is substantially reduced when the person is not able to put them immediately into practice.

Course providers and line managers of staff should be encouraged, where possible, to ensure that the people who are offered places on courses have an imminent need to use the particular software or skill, ie, within the next two or three weeks. Any further delay will substantially reduce the benefit of the training.

Appropriateness of the skills being taught

Many computer trainers and training courses see their objective as to teach the trainees everything there is to know about a piece of software – the A to Z of the Manual approach. This is more often the case when people are sent on externally delivered, off the peg, training courses. External trainers are less likely to be aware of the training needs of the staff in question. The result of this style of training is that staff will waste time learning about features of a package which are completely irrelevant to their job. How many people, for example, who learn about a word processor actually need to know about the automatic creation of indexes and contents pages for a book? On the whole, this is a highly specialized activity in which only a few clerical staff within an institution will be interested.

One of the problems of teaching people more than they need to know is that they may become bored in the training session, or confused about things which do not affect them. This in turn can have a detrimental effect on their ability to absorb the rest of the course.

When planning a course, IT trainers, or those responsible for organizing IT training, should look first at the needs of the people they are training. If, for example, you were teaching secretaries how to use a word processor, the chances are that the first thing on their mind is, 'How can I get this machine to produce a letter?', not 'How many different fonts are available?' or 'Isn't mail merge exciting?' – hopefully, that will come later when they see the relevance of the software to their needs. Alternatively, if the target audience was a group of technicians they may be interested in using the word processor to record the results of an experiment, in which case it would be more sensible to start by teaching them how to use a table to do this. A more appropriate objective for the first session of a word processing course could be: 'At the end of the session the attendees should be able to type, save, re-open and print a simple document relevant to their needs.'

Break down the package and present items in digestible 'bite-size' pieces

Modular programmes consisting of a series of short sessions, approximately two hours each, can help to overcome the problem of people sitting through elements of a course which they feel are irrelevant to their needs. Not everyone who attends a word processing course will want to know how to mail merge letters, therefore it would be appropriate to make this part of the course into an individual session.

When I worked in staff development I established a word processing training programme available to all staff within the institution. In order to make the course appropriate to a wide variety of needs I divided the core skills required to use the package into ten main topics. The training course was then delivered as a series of ten independent two-hour sessions time-tabled over ten weeks. This had the advantage not only of limiting the amount of time people had to concentrate at any one session, but also providing them with the opportunity to practise their newly learnt skills between sessions. Furthermore, staff did not need to attend all ten sessions in the same series. The course was run as a rolling programme and therefore regularly repeated. It was quite possible for people to attend the first five sessions one term and return for the other five at a later time, when they felt more confident with the software. Alternatively, some sessions, which were completely inappropriate for certain people, could be ignored altogether.

It took a while for the culture of the institution to accept the delivery of a course over ten weeks instead of being consolidated into two days, but staff appreciated the opportunity of taking information in at a slower pace and I believe they retained more information and were able to transfer more of their skills back into the workplace than if they had been expected to absorb it all in one concentrated period.

Location of training and training resources

No doubt some institutions still train their staff in computing primarily by sending the trainer to the person and training them at their desk. Apart from being a very expensive use of the trainer's time, it is often not ideal for the person to be trained this way because of the view that they should be available for work at all times. If they are at their desk, then it is assumed that they must be available for work, even if they are clearly engrossed in being trained. Training sessions when I have attempted to assist staff at their workplace have inevitably been riddled with interruptions from other members of staff, phone calls, etc and have, on the whole, been less than satisfactory.

Ideally, staff requiring IT training should be taught in a computer laboratory away from their normal place of work. This may seem obvious, but it is amazing how difficult this can be to achieve. Universities may have computer laboratories available for student use, but how many have got small laboratories of machines dedicated to the training of staff?

Getting the right trainer

This is a sensitive area as there are obviously a large number of skilled IT trainers available, but in my experience finding a trainer who can relate to the needs of support staff within institutions is actually extremely difficult. The usual complaint is that a trainer has been too technical and the trainees have found it extremely difficult to keep up with the jargon and consequently commented that they felt as if the session was a waste of time. Using tutors who are highly capable technically can work well if they are able to communicate at the same level as the trainee, but in many cases they are over-enthusiastic about the product and the machinery and fail to notice that the trainees are experiencing difficulties in understanding. Sometimes it is better to choose tutors who have an obvious empathy with the trainees, perhaps a highly experienced secretary or technician. These people can be difficult to find, and although many turn out to be exceptionally good trainers, others find the ordeal of talking in public too daunting and do not have sufficient confidence to do so.

External tutors will obviously be competent in giving presentations and should be able to train at a level appropriate to the needs of the trainee. The problem with this group, however, apart from their remarkably high fees, is that they probably won't have an understanding of the university work environment. Most external trainers will gear their work to industrial or business needs and consequently their approach to training university staff could be inappropriate.

The problem of finding suitable trainers is one which is very difficult to solve and perhaps the answer is to keep monitoring the reaction of trainees to the trainers on your courses and, when you get a good trainer – make sure you keep them!

What stops us getting IT right

Policy

Most institutions have IT policies that cover the purchasing of equipment, the Internet, or software licence agreements, but how many policy-making committees actually discuss the training required to support the use of IT equipment? Central policies linking a coherent plan of training to the installation of IT systems rarely exist. Institutions rely on individuals to identify their own training needs, which may or may not be in line with the requirements of the department or institution.

Where institutions have a central policy on IT and committees which deal with the co-ordination of IT, there ought to be the inclusion of a body which makes recommendations about staff training and development. When a decision is made to upgrade the centrally supported university word processing software, some account needs to be made of the training implications of that decision if staff, and, in turn, the institution are to maximize the benefit which can be gained by such a change. It is no good moving on to better software to take advantage of additional or improved features if the main staff users of that software aren't informed as to the new features available.

Money and resources

As indicated earlier, money allocated to the training of staff in the use of IT is not commensurate with the money spent on the purchasing and upgrading of equipment. How much more effective could the use of existing IT equipment be if staff were fully trained to use IT to its fullest potential? Resources are required, however, not only to provide trainers, but also to equip adequate, dedicated training areas, and to provide cover for staff, where necessary, whilst they are on training courses. Commitment to these sorts of things has to be a managerial decision made by the central administration of an institution.

Changing the culture

Learning an IT skill requires time to practise. Departments need to create an atmosphere in which allied staff feel it is appropriate to spend time learning how to use their computers, not just by releasing them to attend courses, but by providing realistic opportunities to practise new skills when they are back in the workplace. Perhaps departments or offices could organize regular informal workshops where staff could work on their own documents in the presence of an expert in the subject. Retail outlets and banks have been closing their branches for years at regular times for staff training. Perhaps this is something that universities could learn from business. It seems ironic that a culture dedicated to education seems so reluctant to allow its staff suitable opportunities to acquire knowledge.

Improving the quality of IT training

Harnessing opportunities

Training staff in the use of IT provides an institution with the opportunity of not only developing its staff, but also its systems, its administration and in turn its overall effectiveness. The Internet is heralding a massive change in the way we communicate with each other and this could have a radical effect, for example, on the way students apply for university. Institutions should be looking now at how they can use these facilities to their advantage rather than waiting until the Internet can no longer be ignored and then deciding on an appropriate response. Departments could be pro-active in encouraging their secretaries to become familiar with IT developments, rather than leaving it to the whim and interest of the individual, so that they are encouraged as part of their job to be pro-active, resourceful and enterprising.

Developing staff skills

It is tempting to see IT training in isolation from other types of development and yet the growth of IT understanding may well be dependent on the expansion of other skills. Many people are keen to learn about desktop publishing (DTP) and are encouraged to do so in order to create the departmental newsletter or the staff handbook. Unfortunately training stops after the initial course in DTP. What many people then need is a course in design, layout and presentation. Maybe this way we could avoid the production of documents that use so many fonts and pictures they are impossible to

71

read. Equally, staff who attend courses on databases need to understand something about the nature of data, how data are stored and can be retrieved. One area where I am constantly getting requests for training is in the setting up of databases. What people really need is a course which develops their appreciation of filing and the storage of data and develops their skills to analyse office procedures. If we could develop skills such as these alongside complimentary computer skills we would see some powerful improvements in efficiency and personal development taking place.

Producing better systems and developing standards

Computers themselves are vehicles for creating better administrative systems. Databases and spreadsheets provide efficient ways of storing and analysing data, whilst word processors and desk-top publishers provide the facility to produce better-looking documents at a faster rate than previously possible. Training in all these areas is clearly essential to ensure that the best use is made of these facilities, but it also provides an opportunity to encourage people to use house styles and perform good house-keeping routines, such as regular backups and maintaining security by regular change of passwords. The importance of such activities can be reiterated during training sessions so that people are encouraged to perform regular backup procedures and store data in organized and sensible ways.

What can we hope for in the future?

We can hope that the central administration of universities recognizes the importance of a strategic and planned approach to the delivery of IT training programmes, based on the anticipated needs of the department and staff, combined hand in hand with strategic IT development and not just driven by the desires and enthusiasm of individuals.

We can hope that the quality of the training provided takes into account the key steps to getting it right, making sure suitable tutors are used, and that training is linked to the requirements of the job as well as the individual's desire to learn. We can hope that courses are designed with the needs of the staff in mind and not dictated by the features of the software and the perceived need to know everything about a programme.

We can hope that staff will recognize that appropriate training is that which focuses on the needs of their job and will practise the things they are learning.

Finally, we can hope that universities respond to the rapid changes in technology by introducing training programmes that keep everyone ahead of the game, rather than a step behind.

That's a lot to hope for.

—— 7 ——

The management of pressure and prevention of stress

Debbie Greenwood

Introduction

This chapter, written from a personal viewpoint, will look at the difference between pressure and stress, and will describe some of the most common symptoms of stress and their effect on any employing organization including universities. A number of the causes of stress will be explored as will methods of its reduction and prevention which can be used by individuals and the university as a whole.

I am a 'reformed' stress sufferer and, rather like some reformed smokers, am rather zealous in some of my opinions, but for that I make no apology. My interest has grown over the past few years and I believe that if I can 'come through' stress and out the other side, others can too. The reasons for my stress symptoms I will not recount here, and in any case these are different for each individual. I dealt with the stress myself, but I do feel very strongly that universities as employers should be ensuring that they are pro-active in the stress management of their workforce and that the way forward should not be left to individuals. I know how I felt at the peak of my stress-related illness, which took the form of continual flu-like symptoms, I know how I became 'cured' by changing my attitude to life, by taking a homoeopathic remedy and by taking up a hobby which absorbed my spare time. (Yes, I do now have spare time!) What I did may not work for you, but later in this chapter there are all sorts of ideas, and some of them may just be what you are looking for if you are reading this as an individual who is already suffering from symptoms of stress. If you are reading this as a manager of others, please do be aware of how important your responsibility is to those you manage and consider whether you need to make some changes.

Guidance on stress management by the Health and Safety Executive includes the requirement for pro-active initiatives to control stress in the workplace, and suggests that stress should be viewed as a risk just as much as any other for which assessments are undertaken. Professor Tom Cox, a stress specialist who recently researched into stress for the Health and Safety Executive stated, 'Research findings indicate that workplace stress is an organisational issue rather than one of individual susceptibility or weakness.' Other quotations from the literature show the sheer size of this problem, and the cost to Britain in terms of lost production and money:

> Stress-related illness is now one of the most common causes of certified sick leave involving a loss of 91.5 million working days annually.
>
> (Human Focus International Ltd, 1996)

> . . . stress-related mental illness [causes] a cumulative cost in sick pay, lost production and NHS charges of £7 billion a year.
>
> (Woodham, 1995)

In an article in *People Management* David Littlefield reports that, 'The TUC, which recently surveyed 7000 health and safety officers, found that more than two-thirds said stress was their biggest concern.' So it can be seen that workplace stress is a very real problem not only in terms of staff well-being but also in terms of the efficient running of any organization including universities. Many stress-related problems are foreseeable and this chapter will give individuals, and those who manage others, some practical ideas for stress prevention and management.

The difference between pressure and stress

The terms pressure and stress are sometimes used interchangeably, but they are different. Professor Cary Cooper of the University of Manchester Institute of Science and Technology (UMIST) points out, 'Pressure can stimulate you, is good for you, can make you achieve things. But when that pressure exceeds your ability to cope, then we are talking about stress and stress is not good for you.' So, basically, pressure is good for you and stress is bad! We all need a certain amount of pressure just to give us the motivation to get out of bed in a morning and go about our daily lives. People with too much time on their hands and not enough to occupy their minds can show symptoms of stress, usually in the form of depression, just as much as those people who have too much to do. Stress is often only thought about in terms of people doing too much, but people can also become stressed if they have too little to do. These different types of stress are often referred to by Professor Cooper as 'burn out' and 'rust out' and both types are bad for us. Anne Woodham writes, 'Positive or good stress – sometimes known as eustress – is the kick-start that . . . enables us to take pride in a job well done: . . . It stops life being flat and boring' (1995).

Pressure or eustress is important to individuals, but the problem is that each of us can cope with different amounts of pressure before it becomes stress. Hence, it can be difficult for individuals or their managers to know at what level the 'good' pressure turns into 'bad' stress. What appears to be a highly stressful job may in fact be supplying that individual with just the right amount of motivation to keep them fired up and enthusiastic and not in fact stressed. Conversely, an onlooker watching someone who is working in a mundane or repetitive job may think the job looks very boring and therefore potentially stressful and yet the individual is quite content with the situation and may be getting enough pressure outside work to keep them motivated and interested in life.

As managers of others we have a responsibility to care for the well-being of our staff, to be aware that they may be suffering from stress, to give them the best support possible and to ensure that our management style is not a contributory factor. However, whilst reading the rest of this chapter, please keep in mind that the things that may cause stress, how the symptoms are exhibited and how individuals cope, will be different in each case.

Symptoms of stress

Symptoms of stress can show themselves in many ways and it can therefore be difficult to work out an underlying cause. For example, physical symptoms may become so bad that individuals go to their doctor to ask for some medication and the underlying cause of the problem, which could be stress-related, could be left unexplored. Alternatively, behavioural or emotional symptoms may be causing difficulties at work and could be handled by managers as disciplinary issues, when often what is required is counselling.

The following is a list of physical and behavioural or emotional symptoms which may be associated with stress. (This is not an exhaustive list, nor does it suggest that stress is the only cause, but stress could be borne in mind as a possible cause if symptoms are new, become persistent and there is no other apparent cause.) Most books on stress give varied and comp-rehensive lists of this kind. These types of symptoms can be suffered by anyone in any type of work including both support and academic staff in universities. Some of the symptoms listed below are discussed by Ursula Markham in her book *Managing Stress* (1995).

Physical symptoms

- *Headaches or migraine* – especially if they are suffered at the end of each working day, and a weekend at home seems to make the symptoms disappear until Sunday evening when they start again in anticipation of Monday morning. Individuals could get their eyes checked or consider whether they may have an allergy to certain foods linked to migraine such as coffee, cheese, alcohol or chocolate. However, before seeking help from a doctor it may be as well to take a long hard look at work and consider whether it could be the cause. If there is a work-related problem which is causing the symptoms then both the individual and their manager can do something about it, as shown later in this chapter.

- *Backaches or neckache* – the muscles here soon ache when tense so if you feel this happening throughout a working day try to have a small break, walk round, stretch and massage your own shoulders. Doing this may stop the pain getting a grip in the long term.
- *Indigestion or stomach ulcers* – if you are skipping lunch and eating the wrong type of food so you don't have to leave your desk, or you 'eat on the hoof' whilst working to tight deadlines in a generally stressful environment, you could be in danger of giving yourself digestive problems which could eventually lead to a stomach ulcer.
- *Diarrhoea or irritable bowel syndrome* – diarrhoea is a common symptom in reaction to a sudden crisis and is quite a normal reaction as explained later in this chapter, but if this is happening often you could be in danger of upsetting your system in the long term and the problem becoming more serious.
- *High blood pressure* – this goes up and down naturally throughout the day but if you get stressed on numerous occasions it may rise and stay that way. A fatty diet, lack of exercise and smoking exacerbate the problem.
- *Constant colds or flu or minor infections* – there is evidence that stress can subdue the immune system and physical symptoms appear to go to the individual's 'weak' point, so some people get colds, others sore throats, and women may even get cystitis
- *Constant fatigue* – not the healthy sort of tiredness you feel after a day gardening or a night out dancing, but an exhaustion which does not get better if you have a good night's sleep as you often wake up still feeling tired.

The above are just a sample of physical symptoms but the effect on the university can be major in terms of lost working time. If staff are taking time off work ill and other staff are covering their work, eventually the problem will spiral as those staff in turn feel stressed due to overload. Alternatively a member of staff may come into work but be feeling so ill that their performance is below par and mistakes happen which can lead to accidents, customer complaints or poor morale.

Behavioural and emotional symptoms

Sometimes stress may not show itself in physical symptoms but as a change in the individual's behaviour or emotional state:

- *Excessive drinking or smoking* – this shows itself as a problem when the individual starts to 'need' a drink or a smoke rather than just want one, or they need a drink or a smoke before they can face a particular meeting at work, or straight after an encounter with a particular colleague. Apart from affecting health, the drinking in particular may start to show as a lateness or absence problem if the individual is suffering constantly with hangovers.
- *Excessive eating or loss of appetite* – either of these can be a symptom of stress. The individual who starts to eat excessively is usually gaining some comfort from the food, whilst those who lose their appetites are probably feeling nauseous and can't face food.
- *Making errors or becoming accident prone* – because someone's mind is distracted with a problem, or they are getting too little sleep or feeling generally unwell due to stress, they may start to make errors or have accidents at work.
- *Anger and irritation* – everyone from time to time feels angry or gets irritated with things that are happening around them, but if an individual is always having outbursts of anger or picking arguments with colleagues it could be a sign of stress. Unfortunately if this happens a lot, colleagues may start to disassociate themselves from the individual who may then become isolated and alienated from the rest of the team which can give even more reason for the individual to feel stressed.
- *Loss of affection and interest in self and others* – this often shows at home rather than at work, even if the cause is at work. Due to a depressed state the individual may go off sex, for example, or make excuses to miss a party so they are not put in a position of having to socialize with other people, and they may not care too much about their appearance.

The effect on the university of having employees who are suffering stress and exhibiting it emotionally or behaviourally can be seen in poor team working, lack of communication, misunderstandings, irritability, lack of flexibility, failure to meet deadlines, increases in errors and a rise in accidents. For those staff who work in a high risk area such as a laboratory or workshop, these types of incident can obviously be extremely dangerous. Customer care levels can fall and an atmosphere of 'could not care less' can then soon spread through a workforce. Managers need to be particularly astute and take an interest in the physical and emotional health of their staff.

The data below are taken from MA research in Applied Educational Studies which I undertook in 1994, when I investigated the effect that change was having on support staff in a university in the north of England.

Table 7.1 *How stress manifests itself*

How stress manifests itself	In self (%)	In others (%)
Irritability	65	72
Depression	29	36
Illness	17	41
Poor attitude	14	46
Mistakes	43	37
Customer complaints	12	18
Poor morale	45	58
Resistance to change	8	31
Constant hurrying	62	51
Working long hours	40	30

One of the questions which a cross-section of support staff was asked was whether, in their opinion, they felt that they or others with whom they worked were showing signs of stress. The results are given in Table 7.1, showing the percentage of positive responses in each case, and although the data are now three years old I consider them still to be of some indicative value.

Why do our bodies react to stress in these ways?

The physical reaction to stress is an inherited response to danger from our cave-dwelling days, and is known as the fight or flight response. So the cave-dweller faced with a wild animal had a physical response to the danger that allowed them to either fight it (and hopefully kill and eat it) or run away from the danger. We still get the same responses even if the source of the stress is our boss, our spouse or a traffic warden! Unfortunately now we have to control both the fight and flight instinct and physiological changes in our body are therefore not used as originally intended and hence can cause problems in the long term. The following list of how the body responds to stress is taken from *Stress Management* (Clarke and Palmer, 1994).

- The brain stimulates hormonal changes, including the production of the 'stress hormones' adrenaline and noradrenaline.
- Muscles tense ready for action.
- The pupils of the eye dilate.

- The heart beats faster to get extra blood to the tense muscles and this raises blood pressure.
- The liver releases glucose to provide extra energy for our muscles.
- Our digestive systems shut down so our mouths go dry and our sphincters close.
- We sweat in anticipation of expending extra energy.
- Our immune system slows.

What causes stress in individuals?

People can usually cope with pressure at home or at work, but when the two are making demands at the same time it can be very difficult to deal with.

Causes at home

Although some managers seem to believe that what happens out of work time is completely separate from an individual's working life, in reality people carry round with them anxieties which inevitably have a knock-on effect at work. In 1969 two American researchers put together a scale of what they called 'life events' and gave them a rating as to the degree of stress they placed on individuals. The Holmes-Rahe Social Readjustment Scale attempted to put a score on the amount of stress an individual was experiencing and it is important to note that out of the top ten highest scoring events only one was work-related (dismissal from work); all the others were associated with life traumas like the death of a spouse, divorce and illness. Interestingly, even events which we associate with being nice or good for us have associated stress scores, such as going on holiday or Christmas. Staff who have to care for children or elderly relatives may be showing signs of tiredness or irritability at work, as may staff who have financial worries. Even the most reliable worker can have days when everything goes wrong and they are finding it hard to cope. Lots of little problems like receiving a wrong bank statement, the car breaking down, the central heating not working and forgetting to buy the tickets for the school play can all suddenly add up to changing a normally reliable employee into one who starts to make mistakes or becomes less responsive than usual. So although the main aim of this chapter is to consider how to manage stress at work, managers need to be sympathetic to the life events of their staff.

Causes at work

Those universities that believe they are looking after staff welfare because they offer a counselling service are only really reacting to the problem and not getting to the cause of any work-related issues. The following is a list of some of the most commonly cited stress inducers at work, some of which are discussed in the video and its accompanying booklet entitled *Managing Organisational Stress* (1996) that looks at what organizations can do to prevent employees suffering from stress, and that recommends a pro-active approach to the problem. There is no reason to suppose that such causes are not also apparent in universities; indeed, having spoken in general terms to some people involved with staff welfare and counselling at my own university, it would appear that the causes of stress are remarkably similar to some of those listed below.

- *Overload* - many universities are downsizing and those employees who are left have to manage their own work plus that of others. They 'cope' in the short term by missing lunch breaks, working extended hours and missing holidays, but longer term they become ill and eventually have to take time away from work. This in turn passes the problem onto another staff member and soon the whole workforce in a particular department is affected as surely as if they had been infected by a virus. John Purcell and Sue Hutchinson in *People Management* wrote:

  > it is hard to find evidence that leaner ways of working have positive implications for employees. The evidence suggests that the impact on staff is often negative, particularly when restructuring involves downsizing and re-engineering/slimming and nothing else. Employees work longer hours, stress levels rise, career development opportunities are reduced and morale and motivation fall.
  >
  > (Purcell and Hutchinson, 1996)

  The introduction of new technology in someone's job may also make them feel they are overloaded. Staff can sometimes fear that they are getting 'left behind' if they do not immediately understand some new technology, and such feelings of fear can cause stress.
- *Under-load* – this is not often in terms of the amount of work to be undertaken but the fact that the work has become repetitive and mundane. The introduction of information technology can actually de-skill many jobs, making people into 'number crunchers' and 'button pushers' who can lose contact with their customers and the overall aims of the organization. Boredom ensues and absenteeism rises, and once again this affects the whole team. This is highlighted in two videos, *Managing Organisational Stress*, which shows staff working in a clearing house for Barclays Bank, and *Managing Pressure at Work* which looks at the stress associated with production line working.
- *Uncertainty about the future* – this causes stress for employees as jobs may be threatened, which immediately has a knock on effect to stress levels at home. Communication in such circumstances is often sparse and rumours start, which fire even more anxiety. In the university sector the main problem is short-term contract working when money cannot

always be guaranteed for employment purposes. Many universities are currently re-structuring which again causes anxiety because staff feel they have no control over the eventual outcome of such exercises.

- *Tightly controlled jobs* – it is becoming apparent through research that the stress at work which is most likely to lead to death from heart disease is that caused by lack of control in the job. 'If individuals feel that their behaviour is tightly controlled by external factors they tend to become bored . . . It has been shown that jobs with low decision latitude are related to the highest risk of coronary heart disease.'

- *Inappropriate management ethos and style* – are you condoning long hours by allowing or even expecting staff to work through their lunch, to come in early, stay late or to miss holidays? Do you listen sympathetically if staff have domestic problems or do you assume that any drop in output is a disciplinary issue? Do you punish mistakes and view anyone who is not coping too well as having a weakness that should never be admitted? If as a manager you can answer 'yes' to any of the above, then your style of management is probably causing stress in your staff.

What university management can do to prevent stress

University management should be looking pro-actively at initiatives to control stress in the workplace, and here are a few examples of the action that can be taken:

- *Undertake employee questionnaires* – these can be designed so as to indicate the stress coping abilities of individuals, and also to look at ways of improving the workplace with questions about job design, management style, training, control, communication, career prospects, overload, under-load, involvement, environment and value conflict. Examples of useful questionnaires can be found in *Managing Organisational Stress*. Alternatively, these can be carried out by qualified organizational psychologists. However, it is important if such surveys are undertaken that some action follows to improve any areas identified as causing problems, otherwise employee morale will be worse than if nothing at all had happened. Such questionnaires also need to be conducted in an anonymous and non-threatening way otherwise true feedback will not be given. They must take into account feedback from all grades of staff and any ensuing changes in systems or working practices should be constantly reviewed to evaluate benefits.

- *Look at the job content and design* – are jobs under-loading employees and causing 'rust out' or over-loading them and causing 'burn out'? The amount of control an employee has over their own work is an important factor when managing stress in individuals. Empowering staff to make their own decisions (and not punishing them if they make the wrong ones) helps them to have a real input into their jobs and hence their motivation improves. Overload can sometimes be a problem for managers who try to do too much themselves and do not delegate for various reasons, a common one being fear of letting go of a job. Yet delegation really develops staff, and releases time for the manager to do other things. As *The One Minute Manager Meets the Monkey* states, 'The only way to develop responsibility in people is to give them responsibility.' There is evidence that involving staff in team discussions and decision-making lifts morale and relieves stress caused by lack of control. It is interesting to note that whilst many car manufacturers have moved away from production line working and reorganized the workforce into teams responsible for their own decisions and quality, companies dealing in loan finance, banking and insurance are moving more towards impersonal working practices of high data input using information technology which take away the decision-making parts of the job, increase the need to work to tight deadlines and offer little control over the job by the individual. Such developments in the ways tasks are undertaken in the name of organizational efficiency and productivity are in fact having the reverse effect with staff showing high levels of sickness, absence, turnover and low morale and motivation. University management needs to be aware of such problems when considering how best to perform certain administrative functions.

Other factors within a university which can affect stress levels are a high level of uncertainty related to job security or content, caused by short term contract work and the lack of resources to do the job properly. Occasionally for some staff there may be a high amount of conflict inherent in the job or little opportunity to learn and develop in the job. A number of solutions to these types of situation are given in the following list:

- *Match employee capability and aspirations carefully to the job* – managers need to be mindful that some people can survive on much more pressure before it turns to stress than can others who have a very low stress threshold. Likewise, some jobs might not have the necessary pressure that some people require to keep them fired up and motivated. The level of job pressure needs to be considered during recruitment, appraisal, and promotion interviews. Sometimes there could be external factors which are causing the individual stress already, so giving someone a highly pressured job may make matters worse.
- *Provide training in job skills and coping skills* – such as time management and assertiveness as well as training which enables staff to keep up with new legislation, technology and working practices. Also, there is a need to make managers more aware of the responsibility they have for others. Managers and other staff should be encouraged to attend training courses which cover a range of management skills and coping

strategies which are often offered by their own university's staff development unit. The article 'Stress epidemic hits modern workforce' quoted the results of a Health and Safety survey on stress carried out by the TUC: 'the TUC report lays a considerable part of the blame at the door of modern working methods. . .. The most important step is to educate managers. When they recognise they are over-stressing their staff, they won't do it anymore.' Many managers need training in people management skills, often quite simple things like remembering to say 'thank you' for a job well done, or appreciating how much an employee has tried even if they have been unsuccessful with a piece of work. Time management training is especially important as many subordinates are put under extra pressure trying to keep to deadlines which are too short simply because their managers have not considered the effect of their decisions on their staff's time. The culture of the university may need reviewing. Are managers promulgating an ethos of long and unsociable hours as the only way to get promotion? If this is the case, both management and equal opportunities training may be required.

Offering training to managers in counselling skills should have a positive knock-on effect for their staff. Although many universities already have staff counsellors, a sympathetic ear from an understanding manager who really listens to staff and cares about them as individuals is a good pressure release valve, and may prevent the individual ever having to seek the help of a professional counsellor.

Encouraging managers to communicate effectively, in the right way about the right things and at the right time, will also serve to reduce stress factors in their staff. When concrete facts are missing, especially in times of change, rumours start which spread through unofficial channels – the grapevine. Unfortunately these rumours are rarely accurate and unrest and uncertainty can lead to stress. Many management problems can be traced back to a lack of communication, and many staff development units offer training in this area which managers should be encouraged to attend.

- *Encourage staff to look after themselves physically* – some organizations in the USA have seen huge decreases in absenteeism after instigating 'well employee' schemes: 'General Motors have seen a 40 per cent decrease in absenteeism as a result of health promotion campaigns and Pepsi Cola have achieved a 300 per cent return on their investment in a similar scheme.' (Human Focus International Ltd, 1996) However, as Matthew Mills in his article 'Body and soul' points out, 'The biggest single failing of workplace health promotion is that it does not reach the people who need it most: the lower-paid members of the workforce who suffer more stress, smoke more, drink more, eat more fatty food, are fatter and take less exercise.' He goes on to explain in the article that the unhealthy lifestyle of such staff reflects their inability to satisfy valued needs at work and so they focus on 'treating' themselves with fatty foods, cigarettes and alcohol. His suggestion mirrors some of the points already made in this chapter, that team working, encouraging input to group decisions, gaining praise from their manager, having more control over how they undertake a job and the offer of training and advancement at work are what are really needed, and the health promotion schemes will not work until all the above are in place at the same time.

- *Employ a staff counsellor* – although this is a reactive solution to stress, do offer the opportunity for staff to see a counsellor if it seems necessary. Sometimes there are home-related problems which a staff member will talk to a counsellor about that they would not tell their manager. Alternatively, it may be the manager who is causing the problem and a chance to speak to someone unconnected to the problem could help. Staff and managers should not view going to a counsellor as weak or having failed in some way, and assurances must be given to staff that this type of meeting is totally confidential and the details will not be relayed to the manager, the personnel office or anyone else.

What individuals can do to prevent stress

- *Know yourself* – sometimes we need to take a step back from all that is going on around us to check that what we are doing fits in with our goals and values. If you have been feeling particularly stressed or even just experiencing a nagging feeling that something is not quite right it could be appropriate to set a small amount of time aside to consider whether your life is on the right track. An audiotape package entitled *The Balancing Act* takes the listener through the process of creating a 'life balance wheel' in which you draw a pie chart and try to decide how you are currently spending your time. There are six headings: personal physical (anything to do with your physical state of health including sleeping, exercise, eating and also your appearance); personal emotional (such things as quiet thought, reading for pleasure, religious worship, hobbies); family and loved ones (including very close friends); earning a living (including any education you are taking which is job-related and travel to and from work); domestic (housework, gardening, shopping, decorating); and time spent on other activities with/for others (time with acquaintances rather than close friends, doing things for others such as Parent Teacher Association, running a youth group, running cubs or brownies, collecting for charities). If you can't decide where something fits, think of the motivational thought behind it, hence gardening for some may be a household chore but for others a hobby. Similarly, running a youth group may be a hobby or it may be something you feel you 'ought' to be doing for others. Try to fit into your pie chart the percentage of time you are currently spending on all these activities and have a look at the result. Then draw another pie chart and mark out how you would like to spend time. A knee-jerk reaction to this question is usually 'give up work', but be realistic! If you have not won the lottery you may not be able to give up work completely. You could, however, give serious consideration to the number of hours you are currently working; could you still survive financially with a change of lifestyle if you were to work less hours? If you find that in any area of your pie chart there is a big discrepancy between how you actually spend your time and what you would like it to be, you may have highlighted a source of stress. Another common area that comes to light is that people would prefer to be spending longer with close friends and family than they are currently. If this is the case for you, ask if there is anything at all in the rest of the chart that you could give up to free some time for what you really want from life.

Think about your values too, what you hold to be good and bad, right and wrong. As Anne Woodham says, 'If the situation in which we find ourselves, our job or our relationships, is out of kilter with these attitudes, then we feel de-valued ... the misfit is a nagging and destabilising source of strain' (1995).

- *Develop support systems* – people usually need other people around them who can support them in various ways. Ask yourself if you have someone with whom you can relax and have fun, someone who makes you laugh, someone who will listen to your concerns, someone to give you wise counsel, someone who pushes you to achieve, someone who unconditionally approves of you, someone who will give you feedback. These preferably are not all the same person, and in some cases do not have to be a person; the unconditional approval, for example, may come from a dog or cat. If you cannot bring to mind people who can support you, can you start to nurture some relationships with a view to this in the future? Don't forget it will not be 'all take' on your part, you may be able to offer similar support to them.

- *Look at your lifestyle* – some of you may now be thinking 'here we go again, being told to be healthy', but a healthy body really can make a big difference in helping to keep a healthy state of mind. If you are feeling shattered at the end of a busy and frustrating day at work, possibly the last thing you want to do is to undertake exercise. Falling asleep on the sofa after a few glasses of wine may sound much better! Yet, if you can make yourself exercise (anything you enjoy, gardening, walking, swimming, dancing, it does not have to be a 'tortuous' aerobics class), you will get some oxygen pumping through your veins and quickly start to feel the benefit. Surprisingly, having a tired body after exercising seems to awaken the mind, and although you will feel tired, it is a healthy bodily tiredness, not that sluggish feeling that comes from a stressed mind. A good diet also helps; try not to eat too much fat, sugar or salt which can lead to obesity, heart problems and raised blood pressure. The problem of poor diet is often exacerbated by rushing about and not making time to eat healthily, grabbing snacks which are usually high in fat and salty or sugary. Do not deprive yourself completely, however; the odd bar of chocolate or glass of wine can make you feel as if you are treating yourself, which is important. Watch the alcohol intake, however, since over a period of time you may become even more tired through its effects, especially if you get hangovers. Smoking of course is bad for you, and it is a fallacy that it calms your nerves. 'The greater the stress, the more cigarettes a smoker will puff. And yet the chemical changes that nicotine produces in the body include the release of stress hormones adrenaline and noradrenaline. Smoking actually makes stress symptoms worse.'

- *Develop new skills and strategies* – such as assertiveness, time management, how to cope with change, and keep up to date with new working methods and technology. Many university staff development units offer workshops on these topics so get yourself booked on one, or do some reading on the subjects. Some people worry that by attending such workshops they are admitting to a weakness, but you are merely acknowledging an area that can be developed and are likely to be a stronger person for admitting it and doing something about it. Assertiveness training involves defending your own rights while respecting the rights of others, and will help you to say 'no' nicely, but mean it! By being assertive you can start to develop your self-esteem and your work role. 'Often you avoid the stress situations, such as speaking up at a meeting or asking for more challenging assignments . . . thus limiting your work and reducing opportunities for growth and advancement.' (Fernsterheim and Baer, 1989)

Time management is another essential skill to develop to reduce your risk of succumbing to stress, and is so inextricably linked to assertiveness it is almost impossible to talk about one without the other. Make yourself less available, book time for yourself in your diary and again learn to say 'no'. 'Time is a vital resource and we all need to guard against its misuse. If you find you are taking work home in the evening or working late, you are probably not relaxing fully and so getting stressed because you are too tired to concentrate at work. Then you may feel you haven't enough time to get your work done properly. And so the vicious circle goes on.' (Clarke and Palmer, 1994)

Workshops and books on coping with change can help you to keep things in perspective and avoid letting worry and resentment get the better of you and thus be a cause of stress. In the book *How to Stop Worrying and Start Living*, Dale Carnegie quotes the prayer about coping with change written by D Reinhold Niebuhr,

God grant me the serenity
To accept the things I cannot change,
The courage to change the things I can;
And the wisdom to know the difference.

If you are worried that you are on a short-term contract or could be made redundant in the future, you are not alone, as unfortunately job insecurity is a fact of life today, not only in universities but in all walks of life. As an article in *People Management*, 'Managing to look after Number One' stated, 'the demise of the "job for life" is making workers ill', but if you are flexible in what you will do and are willing to keep up with new technologies and techniques so that you have a wide portfolio of talents to offer prospective employers, you should be in a much stronger position to keep or find work than people who have given up learning new knowledge and skills.

- *Avoid self-inflicted stress* – which can be caused by negative self-talk; don't be too critical of yourself. If you make a mistake at work do not think 'I'm so stupid, no one else would have done that'; think instead, 'I had better put that right and learn from that mistake.' Be kind to yourself, try to treat yourself as a friend. We are often much more critical of ourselves than we would be with a friend. As Dale Carnegie says, 'Eight words can transform your life: "Our life is what our thoughts make it."'

- *Explore alternative therapies* – there are all sorts of therapies around that can help you to prevent or cope with stress. Hypnotherapy, acupuncture, yoga, aromatherapy, reflexology and homoeopathy are becoming popular and are sometimes being sponsored by employers who recognize their benefits. In the article 'Alternative ways to take out stress', Siobahn Butler, a human resources manager at Cable Midlands, describes some of the workshops on offer to staff which include aromatherapy and reflexology sessions, and reports that sickness absence is falling and that, 'There is a genuine feeling that the company cares about the welfare of its employees.'

Homoeopathy is particularly useful if you are suffering from ongoing physical symptoms which might not so far have been diagnosed as being caused by stress. A typical first appointment could take around two hours, during which time the homoeopath will explore who you are as a person and what makes you 'tick', as well as concentrating on the specific symptoms from which you are suffering. Ill health is viewed by a homoeopath as an expression of disorder within the whole body and is treated by stimulating the individual's vitality, hence stress-related problems can be eased quite significantly. Alternatively, simply teaching yourself how to relax can be most beneficial. Sit comfortably, close your eyes and let your mind drift and your muscles go heavy, and do it in your office in a lunch time if necessary!

Conclusion

The Health and Safety Executive have realized that stress is a very real issue to British workers and that it should be treated as a health and safety issue like any other hazard. Universities need to be pro-active in their approach to preventing employee stress and not merely re-active in providing sick pay or counsellors when staff succumb to stress. The culture of the university and its managers has to be sympathetic to the causes of stress and not treat it as a weakness, but even if your organization fails to act there are many things that you as an individual can do for yourself to keep stress from overtaking your life.

I did it, so can you!

References

Blanchard, K, Oncken Jr, W and Burrows, H (1990) *The One Minute Manager Meets the Monkey*, Collins, London.

Butler, S (1996) 'Alternative ways to take out stress', *People Management*, vol. 2, no. 10, 16 May, pp. 43–4.

Carnegie, D (1989) *How To Stop Worrying and Start Living*, Cedar Books.

Clarke, D and Palmer, S (1994) *Stress Management* (training package), Cambridge: National Extension College Trust Ltd.

Epstein, B (1988), *The Balancing Act* (audiotape), CareerTrack, USA.

Fensterheim, H and Baer, J (1989) *Don't Say 'Yes' When You Want to Say 'No'*, Futura Publications Ltd, Aylesbury.

Froggatt, H and Stamp, P (1991) *Managing Pressure at Work*, BBC Training Videos, London.

Hallier, J and Lyon, P (1996) 'Managing to look after Number One', *People Management*, vol. 2, no. 9, 2 May, pp. 38–9.

Human Focus International Ltd (1996) *Managing Organisational Stress* (video and workbook package) Surrey.

Littlefield, D (1996) 'Stress epidemic hits modern workforce', *People Management*, vol. 2, no. 21, 24 October, p. 15.

Markham, U (1995) *Managing Stress: The Stress Survival Guide for Today*, Element Books Ltd, Dorset.

Mills, M (1996) 'Body and soul', *People Management*, vol. 2, no. 19, 26 September, pp. 36–8.

Purcell, J and Hutchinson, S (1996) 'Lean and mean', *People Management*, vol. 12, no. 20, 10 October, pp. 27–33.

Woodham, A (1995) *Beating Stress at Work*, Health Education Authority, London.

—8—

It's not just courses: other ways of developing higher education support staff

Anne Sibbald

Changing occupational and skill requirements

Universities and colleges are largely staff-intensive and have operated successfully over a great number of years with teams of support or allied staff to provide a professional back-up to the academe. I use the term 'teams' loosely, for I suggest that previous generations of academics would not necessarily view these staff as working alongside them, but as subordinates. This view is gradually changing and in 1987 Fender noted; 'A key requirement for success is the recognition that training is a management responsibility. A commitment by everyone who has management responsibilities is essential'.

Demographic changes indicate that the 1990s have required us to meet the skill needs with an older workforce and a reduced in-flow of young first-time recruits who have normally been relied upon to bring new skills to higher education. In addition to demographic change there are other factors which have to be considered; changes in occupational and skill requirements are already taking place and will continue; patterns of organizations and employment are changing (see Figure 8.1); additional challenges will continue throughout the 1990s and beyond.

It would appear that:

- there has been a job growth in the service sector, with a marked decline in other sectors, particularly manufacturing;
- demand for those with management, professional and technical skills is increasing, while for employees in lower level manual occupations they are decreasing;

- available occupational projections suggest continued growth, further shifts from primary and manufacturing industries to the service sector, and a similar rapid growth in demand for managers, administrators, professional, technical and personal service staff.

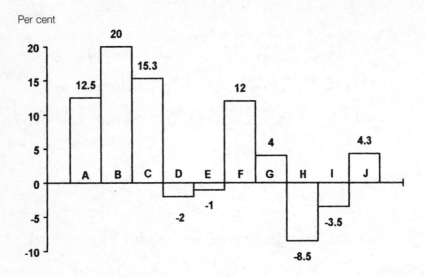

Figure 8.1   *UK occupational projections, percentage change 1990*
(A – Managers & administrators; B – professional occupations;
C – associated professional; D – clerical and secretarial; E – craft and
skilled manual; F – personal and protective services; G – sales occupations;
H – plant and machine operators; I – other occupations;
J – whole economy)

Source: Institute for Employment Research, 1990

Challenges for training and staff development

It is my belief that the success of university and college departments, and consequently the organization itself, will ultimately be a challenge for the manager. It is their responsibility to harness the talents and enthusiasm of staff and nurture it accordingly. Increasingly, younger staff have an expectation that they will be given delegated responsibility and therefore managers, at all levels, must ensure that programmes of training and management development are put in place.

Obviously, heads of departments must have a clear vision of their own plan, with specific and achievable goals, realistic time-frames, and all staff should be aware of the plan. Ownership of the plan could be devolved to staff and a good communication channel would need to be established in order to allow the head (the manager) to demonstrate their leadership role, the need for consistency and demonstrable commitment. The plan should clearly state the future need in terms of training and development and focus on both the skills and development needs of staff (not just courses) that will aid the staff development department in formulating a comprehensive and coherent staff development plan, in line with the organization's strategy.

Examples of alternative development activities

Developing in-house trainers

One of the first tasks I was faced with in my new role in staff development at Heriot-Watt back in 1990 was to deliver a programme of customer care training. Initially, I thought, bring in a consultant, train the receptionists and that will be that! How wrong I was and, fortunately, I was on a fast learning curve at the time. (Otherwise, I would have been demolished by a rather frugal budget, very quickly.) The first two areas of demand were the catering and residencies section and the library. The total numbers of staff were around 260, but many of them were part-time. This presented our first challenge, in that we had to set about producing programmes to suit various time-frames.

At the outset, therefore, I set about recruiting my internal trainers. We identified eight members of staff whom we thought would do a good job (drawn from a range of service areas in the university, including careers, library, conference office, cleaning services, personnel, catering and residences) and set up a training programme, using consultants who were familiar with the higher education (HE) system. The programme was intensive, involving three days of training, including use of Closed Circuit Television (CCTV), and was followed by trainers running a mock-programme before a hand-picked audience who gave the trainers objective feedback. (The latter, interestingly enough, was harsher than any audience has ever been since that initial pilot programme.)

I believe my own development took a major leap forward throughout this programme; I learnt that staff are terrified by CCTV; that my expectations for those with heavy day jobs were unrealistic; in the first six months trainers were delivering eight workshops a month! Unbelievably, most of these trainers are still working with me seven years down the line!

On the positive side, we succeeded in producing a programme of three half-days for each member of staff and seven of the trainers provided this training on a paired basis over a period of eighteen months. (One of the trainers withdrew during the training, as the work appeared to be too awesome.) The trainers worked to a very high standard and received positive feedback from the participants. In recent years, we have extended the programme to cover many other departments and have added six more trainers to our team. Each receives a small honorarium and a meal out at Christmas for their endeavours!

Such was the success of this model of training and development that we have extended the in-house trainers to cover IT skills, including basic and advanced word processing, Excel and PowerPoint training and work is underway to produce database workshops. Once again, the trainers deliver workshops in pairs, which helps to reduce stage-fright as well as adding interest for the audience. Over the last three years this model has been extended to cover academic staff development.

Who benefits?

My answer is, everyone! The trainers have gained a great deal in that they develop their own skills in writing training materials, and in delivery. Further, they enjoy the status of being an in-house expert or facilitator. Many have remained as trainers because they enjoy the interpersonal nature of the task. The staff benefit by having in-house trainers who understand their culture and their problems, but also from having the trainer remain on site.

Finally the university is very much a beneficiary, in that this method is an extremely prudent method of delivering large amounts of training. It retains the experts, who incidentally act as disciples for the staff development unit and, judging by the level of interest from other institutions, must send out positive signals about the commitment to customer care in particular.

My only words of caution would be in initiating such programmes and the levels of commitment expected from trainers must be established with the individual and their respective head of department. Although I had no rejections, it was not all plain sailing with certain heads and therefore the secretary of the university assisted by negotiating meaningful contracts with staff, in order for them to be released to undertake training for the unit. It is essential that staff are adequately trained before commencing their delivery programme and although no-one particularly enjoys CCTV, it has been highly beneficial, mainly because the training services of a sensitive external consultant are employed to run this session.

Job secondments or job shadowing

During my first year or so in staff development I first became aware of the fact that support staff rarely left their home institution, sometimes not straying from their own departments, unlike their academic counterparts, many of whom can be more away than within! From a staff development point of view there seemed, to me, to be no logic to this fact and the national UCoSDA annual conference proved to be an excellent opportunity to further my thoughts on the matter.

I was fortunate to meet Jenny Grant of Surrey University, which was for some time undertaken job secondments for many groups of support staff, including administrators, secretaries and technical staff. Such is the maturity and acceptance of the scheme that they frequently have staff travelling to Holland, USA and more recently Australia.

The Scottish universities invited Jenny to speak to a group of staff developers in order to inform them of the advantages of the scheme and to endeavour to establish similar programmes for Scotland. Heriot-Watt has piloted three secondments from the technical grades. Each had a specific agenda to address and to a large extent were successful in achieving them. Here are two examples with positive and negative outcomes discussed.

A chief technician in a large engineering department, in his mid-fifties, who is an excellent craftsman but has recently been required to undertake a number of clerical tasks occasioned by the restructuring of a large, merged department. With the appointment of a professional administrator who has taken over this paperwork, he now feels demotivated and deskilled.

This member of staff visited an appropriate English university, and the shadow department was well organized and similar in many ways to his home base. The secondee was provided with a number of issues which were to be addressed during the visit and to aid this he was furnished with a camera. The outcome was a full report on procedures, including a visual display, demonstrating how the laboratories and work areas were organized. Two months later, the secondee had to host his English counterpart and establish a programme of activity and development for him during his visit.

Positives: The secondee returned feeling of value to Heriot-Watt and commented that it was 'the first time he had been sent on a plane on business'. This initiative helped to address the individual's feeling of self-worth, especially in terms of subordinate colleagues. The secondee learnt a lot by having to focus on key issues when in the host institution and enjoyed being able to explore how things might be undertaken differently. Equally, having to host the counterpart was a very useful exercise in itself.

Negatives: The secondment was felt not to be long enough in duration and five full days were recommended as a minimum. The head of department needs to have a plan to follow up on the outcomes of such a visit and, in this particular case, the job required a complete re-write and full discussions with other staff.

The secondee, having gained a lot from the visit, should have shared this with colleagues immediately on his return and although this was done, it was rather too late in the day to be helpful.

A senior graded technician in a recently merged engineering department who has been given new administrative duties, including addressing results of changes in engineering regulations.

This secondee was sent to a similar technological English university for a week, with the specific intention of establishing how they had addressed this problem.

Positives: The outcomes were highly satisfactory in that the secondee wrote an extremely full and meaningful report, as well as making contact with fellow colleagues and is now suitably motivated and wishes to pursue further qualifications.

Negatives: On this occasion, a period longer than a week would have been beneficial.

Establishing a specialist training fund

The establishment of a specialist training fund has overwhelmed us with its results. The fund amounts to approximately £10,000 per annum and allows staff to reflect upon their own continuing professional development whilst seeking funds from the university to jointly pursue qualifications.

Departments hold funds for use in developing staff. In practice the staff who usually benefit from this are mainstream academics. Support staff have been the poor relations. Funds to academics have been utilized mainly in the area of research, with teaching and learning having taken a back seat. On the advice of one of my academic advisers some six years ago, and in the hope of stimulating academic staff to attend development sessions relating to teaching and learning, the unit set aside a tranche of money from the staff development budget and staff were invited to make bids accordingly. We have always taken a holistic view at Heriot-Watt and so the fund was open to all staff. In the event, it proved to be support staff who showed a keener interest in development initiatives and so it worked almost by default.

At the outset, many technical staff expressed the desire to attend one-day workshops on new skills and technologies but the largest level of interest lay with the secretarial and clerical staff who were keen to pursue further qualifications, especially those at Higher National Diploma level, with language included.

How did it work in practice?

A number of advisory panels, each of which represents the needs of different staff groupings, exist at Heriot-Watt and it fell to these panels to prioritize bids. Each bid had to have the support of the head of department in writing and a commitment to pay 50 per cent of the fees (the staff development unit giving financial support up to a maximum of £300 per person). In addition, heads of departments were encouraged to give support in a number of other ways including day-release, time off for residential weekends and study leave.

This mode of operation has, I believe, stimulated heads of departments into reflecting on the training and development needs of support staff whilst the assistance from the centre has added impetus to their commitment, without over-burdening them financially. Staff too feel that they can add to their skills and change direction; either upwards or sideways, into a new career path. Topics covered have ranged widely, from counselling to certificates in staff training and development.

The downside at the moment is that all the demands cannot be met. Many staff wish to pursue Open University qualifications, MBAs, advanced IT courses and language tuition. Unfortunately, this demand upon the current resource is too great. I hope that this will be revised by the Executive and might be regarded as an investment in the further development of its most valuable resource.

Staff development involvement

I have alluded previously to the panel system which operates at Heriot-Watt University. I believe that this system works reasonably efficiently and effectively and would commend the initiative as a good way of involving a very large and diverse workforce in staff development and related issues.

Heriot-Watt has a total of 1500 staff, approximately 1000 of whom are support staff (administrative, clerical, computing, library, manual, secretarial and technical). Initially, we established three panels, these being academic, technical and secretarial and clerical. More recently, we have established a further two, manual and administrative/research/computing and library. Each panel is chaired by a professorial or equivalent colleague with their membership being widely spread across the university, including cross-faculty and trade union representation. The panels meet at least once per term and have specific tasks, for example, the monitoring of the trainee technician scheme, setting up training needs analyses programmes (for which individuals have specific responsibility), identifying particular needs, prioritizing bids for the specialized training fund and helping with the design and servicing of conferences.

This mode of operation has served as a trailblazer for a number of other events. Heriot-Watt ran the first Scottish Chief Technicians' Course, swiftly followed by Glasgow University, who ran a similar course. This has raised the expectations of the senior technicians and now forms part of the regular calendar of events in Scotland. A similar event is planned for members of the support staff who are regarded as having the potential to progress into a leadership role. Support staff have been involved in all stages of the planning and facilitation of these events. Other programmes of development are held throughout Scotland and include, for example, Robert Gordon University in Aberdeen hosting an annual conference for secretarial staff which has established a new opportunity for a group of staff who once upon a time were barely able to leave their desks, let alone their institutions.

A spin-off from the residential courses has been the formation of a support group, the Office Support Staff Network (OSSN). These are a group of enthusiasts who have worked together and arranged a programme of events for the secretarial staff. They meet once per term and have guest speakers. For example, one of Heriot-Watt's academics talked about stress (his research topic) and the occupational health doctor is to talk about women's health issues. The staff development unit's contribution is to pay for the sandwich lunch!

By way of the university's appreciation, the OSSN formation groups were recently in receipt of the prestigious Principal's Award for Excellence. This award is made annually by the Principal to support staff who have made a significant contribution to the good working of the organization. This group has achieved this because events organized here have attracted extensive support. Approximately half the secretarial population has attended each event and more recently the committee were invited to share their experiences with a similar group at another university.

An investment or a cost?

A study by the Cranfield School of Management (1990) and the consulting group Price Waterhouse attempted to discover the main issues confronting human resource practitioners, and some 6000 companies and public sector bodies were examined in the UK and other European countries. The survey covered a range of questions including human resource strategies, attitudes towards recruitment, pay, benefits, employee relations, work patterns and training and development. With regards to training and development, some important findings emerged, as follows:

- personnel responsibility is increasingly being delegated to line management, and in particular, as part of that function, the training and development of both shop-floor workers (or their equivalent) and managers;
- organizations throughout the countries covered by the survey have increased significantly their investment in training, particularly with respect to managers and professional staff, although there is little evidence of the systematic evaluation of such training;
- although the survey reveals that between 60 and 90 per cent of the responding companies systematically analyse their training needs, it also reveals a lack of knowledge among human resource professionals of how much their companies are actually spending on the training and development of their staff;
- managers are currently being trained across a wide spectrum of what can be called 'people management' skills and it is 'people management' which is expected to dominate in almost all of the countries surveyed;

- apart from the traditional reaction responses of trainees and their line managers to particular training experiences, the validation and evaluation of training tend to be informal and unsystematic.

I believe these findings are still relevant. Increasingly, I have viewed in my own institution the desire for department-specific workshops and seminars, often because one person attending a course can feel very isolated on his/her return to the workplace. In cases where the involvement of the entire department is crucial to the success of the investment in time and financial resource, the days of applying courses in a scatter-gun approach are, in my view, long gone.

The outcome for the trainer or staff developer will be to dramatically heighten their involvement and commitment in a true partnership with line management in the examination of business and strategic objectives and the assessment, both in the short and the long term, of the training implications. This is arguably the most effective way of ensuring that training and development activities are truly congruent with corporate objectives. A list of staff development activities, other than courses, that might assist this process are shown:

- coaching by a senior colleague;
- secondments;
- temporary membership of a task force or working party;
- custom designed projects;
- job rotation or shadowing;
- standing in;
- in-house informal seminars/workshops/discussion groups;
- tutoring by peers;
- tutoring of peers;
- visits;
- sitting in as an observer on committees and *ad hoc* meetings;
- committee work inside and outside the university;
- training junior staff;
- self-paced open learning and distance learning;
- representing the department/faculty/university in the wider community;
- giving formal or informal presentations;
- organizing formal events;
- guided reading;
- learning resources (libraries, media services, etc);
- learning contracts or portfolio approaches.

Benefits of evaluation

Most, if not all of us, have been distributing what are commonly called 'happy sheets' at the end of courses. I believe these have some worth but, as with student questionnaires, they only tell part of the story. For example, trainees may have witnessed a superb performance, but did the day out increase their long-term learning or effectiveness in the organization?

Trained skills must be transferable. Too often they are seen as being of short-term benefit to an organization, since the long-term benefit might be gathered by other employers. This is a short-sighted view. Many problems have been caused in Britain by narrow training schemes and programmes which do not allow people the flexibility to move from section to section within organizations. In some cases, redundancies have resulted in one part of an organization, while there are unfilled vacancies in similar areas of the same organization.

Added value cannot be overlooked. In the case of the internal trainers, IT training alone saved the University of Heriot-Watt *circa* £60,000 last year but the main benefit to the university is the retention of excellent trainers, who are highly motivated. Equally, this base of personnel adds to the learning culture where training and development have become demand-led rather than supply-driven. An organization requires enthusiastic leaders at all levels who give commitment and support, coupled to the allocation of adequate resources to train and develop its workforce. Participative leadership in a learning culture, with goal-orientated strategic plans, will bring about pro-active solutions with the staff developer playing a key role, in turn both attracting and developing staff through to the millennium and beyond.

References

Cranfield School of Management (1990) *The Price Waterhouse Cranfield Project on International Strategic Human Resource Management*, Bedford.

CVCP (1987) *Report of the Fender Committee: Investing in People*, CVCP, London.

'Labour advise force outlook to 2001', *Employment Gazette*, April 1990.

Davies, A (1992) *Demographic Change: Implications for the 1990's*, Gower, Aldershot.

Fricker, J (1992) *Training for Change: An Investment in People*, Gower, Aldershot.

The Investors in People initiative and its implications for support staff in higher education

Bob Thackwray

Does this mean the gardener has to read the strategic plan?

(Chambers, 1996)

Introduction

In this chapter I describe the Investors in People (IIP) national standard, its origins and its application within the higher education sector. The national standard is divided up into four complementary principles. Each principle is supported by a number of indicators. The 23 indicators are examined in relation to higher education later in this chapter. The four principles are:

- *Commitment*: an Investor in People makes a commitment from the top to develop all employees to achieve its business objectives;
- *Planning*: an Investor in People regularly reviews the needs and plans for the training and development of all employees;
- *Action*: an Investor in People takes action to train and develop individuals on recruitment and throughout their employment;
- *Evaluation*: an Investor in People evaluates the investment in training and development to assess achievement and improve future effectiveness.

Investors in People is increasingly being recognized as the major standard for good practice in the development of people to achieve business success. It is arguably the most important initiative in the area of general continuing professional development in recent times. At the time of writing, well over 6000 organizations have been recognized as Investors in People. Over 21,000 organizations have committed themselves to becoming recognized and are actively working towards meeting the requirements of the national standard. Recognized and committed organizations together comprise 31 per cent of the total UK workforce.

Interest is not just confined to the UK. In early 1996 Investors in People was launched in Australia where at the time of writing six organizations had achieved recognition. Although not officially launched in any other countries, a great deal of interest is being shown elsewhere in Europe and in the USA.

Its impact on higher education is significant and its potential impact even more so. Several UK higher education institutions have been recognized as Investors in People. Many more have recognized departments or autonomous units and still more are currently 'on the journey'. Over 100 higher education institutions have declared themselves to be at some stage in actively implementing Investors in People, from the initial diagnostic stage to actual recognition (HEQC/UCoSDA,1995, 1996).

History and development

The Investors in People process was triggered by the knowledge that Britain's existing workforce held fewer qualifications than most of our major competitors. One report, *Training in Britain 1987*, published by the Training Agency branch of the Employment Department, drew attention to the fact that although £18 billion per annum was spent on training, employers in Great Britain did not spend as much as their competitors and the skills gap was widening. There were a number of groups with an interest in addressing this situation. The key players were: the National Training Task Force (NTTF); the Confederation of British Industry (CBI); and the Employment Department. The CBI established a task force, led by Sir Bryan Nicholson. The task force report, *Towards a Skills Revolution*, introduced the concept of an Investor in Training. The report, in addition to outlining ten principles for an Investor in Training, also set a number of targets. One of the most significant was that 'by 1995 at least half of all medium-sized and larger companies should qualify as Investors in Training as assessed by the relevant Training and Enterprise Council'(TEC). (This target would later be amended, replacing Investors in Training with Investors in People, after some considerable amount of research on naming the initiative had been undertaken!)

At the CBI Conference in 1989 where the report was presented, the then Secretary of State for Employment, Norman Fowler, proposed that the NTTF work with the CBI and with other business and training organizations, including TECs, to develop an action programme. A group of 'practitioners' was established and included representatives from a number of government departments, TEC Chief Executives, CBI, Institute of Personnel Management (IPM), Institute of Training and Development (ITD), Trades Union Congress (TUC), National Council for Vocational Qualifications (NCVQ), Industry Training Organizations and the Association of British Chambers of Commerce. Their remit was to consider and develop proposals and make recommendations to the NTTF sub-group. Over the next six to nine months the action programme concept was moulded and developed. The idea of a standard based on good practice was mooted.

The criteria chosen for the standard were based on the best practice of selected employers. Best practice, as defined within the standard, arose from the in-depth study of a wide range of successful organizations drawn from all sectors of the economy. It was also influenced considerably by the CBI's ten principles for an Investor in Training and took into account lessons learned from the Employment Department's employer initiatives such as the National Training Awards and Business Growth Training.

An over-riding principle was that organizations should not feel that this initiative was a government-driven bureaucratic exercise or a top-down initiative. Organizations themselves must be allowed to meet the criteria in a way that offered clearly perceived and measurable benefits to their individual activities. An early outline of the criteria was drawn up and Price Waterhouse were commissioned to develop the framework.

From July 1990 some of the early TECs and the then residual Area Offices of the Training Agency and the Office for Scotland were invited to pilot the concept with employers in their areas. These pilots were the first stage in selling the potential benefits of the initiative to the people who would eventually have to run with it. The pilots met with mixed levels of success but in general confirmed significant interest levels amongst employers.

Whilst the pilots were progressing, market research was being undertaken to establish the name. The outcome was presented to the NTTF Sub-Group together with a logo. Their decision resulted in the current logo and the name Investors in People. The name was announced and the national standard launched by Michael Howard, Secretary of State for Employment, at the CBI Conference in Glasgow in November 1990. Price Waterhouse, meanwhile, were developing the assessment framework. This work, together with the continuation of the pilots and an invitation to TEC staff to identify companies whom they felt to be close to meeting the criteria, culminated in around 40 companies being assessed during the summer of 1991. Of these, 28 met the standard and were subsequently recognized at a media event held in London on 16 October 1991. In addition to recognizing the first Investors in People, the event also provided a summary of progress to date and listed those companies who had made a commitment to work towards the standard.

Early concerns voiced by employers included potential bureaucracy, the quality of the assessors and the challenge of applying the standard on a national basis. The twin terrors of bureaucracy and interference still surface today but if there is a culture that sees the benefits of continuous professional development for all employees these concerns are groundless.

At the end of 1992 the NTTF ceased to exist but the role of the sub-group set up by Sir Brian Wolfson was widened to cover all aspects of employer investment (in their workforce). This enhanced role included:

- oversight of the further development of the initiative;
- recognition of those TECs who had been assessed by national assessors as having met the criteria;
- recognition of some large and multisited organizations who had chosen to be assessed nationally.

The establishment of Investors in People UK

The sub-group continued to operate until the end of June 1993. On 1 July a new body, Investors in People UK, was established and chaired by Sir Brian Wolfson. The membership of this body was appointed by the Secretary of State following consultation with the TEC movement. It was also announced that this body would have an executive arm, a private company limited by guarantee, which would take over some of the work that had previously been undertaken by officials in the Employment Department.

The role of Investors in People UK is to:

- be a protector of the national standard;
- market and promote Investors in People nationally;
- provide a national assessment and quality assurance service.

Investors in Scotland

Scotland has Local Enterprise Companies (LECs) instead of TECs. Although LECs carry out the same basic functions as TECs they also have an enhanced role as they also carry out the functions of either Scottish Enterprise or Highlands and Islands Enterprise. The decision was taken early in the development of Investors in People to set up a separate company, Investors in People Scotland Ltd, who would carry out assessments on behalf of the LECs. All the work prior to assessment is carried out by the LECs.

Investors in Northern Ireland

Northern Ireland has neither TECs nor LECs. Their role is carried out by the Training and Employment Agency – a government agency. The Agency's involvement with Investors in People began in early 1993 with their first recognition of companies as Investors in People in October of that year. The Agency carries out the same role as TECs in England and Wales.

Investors in People in higher education

The Further and Higher Education Act 1992 took further education out of public sector local authority control and abolished the binary system of polytechnics and universities as separate providers of higher education. The former polytechnics were established as (the 'new') universities in their own right alongside the 'old' universities and both became subject to the same Higher Education Funding Councils from 1 April 1993. (These superseded the former University Funding Council, set up in 1989, and the Polytechnics and Colleges Funding Council (PCFC).)

This began a new era whereby the unit cost of the 'old' university teaching provision became directly comparable with that achieved by the ex-polytechnics and these 'new' universities could compete for research resources for the first time. In tandem with these changes, several mechanisms have been set in train for monitoring and regularly reviewing the standard and quality of all aspects of university education. These include:

- the CVCP's Academic Audit Unit (AAU) from October 1990 (now subsumed into the Higher Education Quality Council: shortly to be wound up with its functions transferred to the newly established Quality Assurance Agency for Higher Education);
- the teaching quality assessments from 1993 onwards undertaken by the respective Higher Education Funding Councils for England, Scotland and Wales; and
- the research assessment exercises in 1992 and 1996, which directly link funding with the assessments made.

Therefore the higher education sector over the past 15 years has been subject to increasing government intervention culminating in the promotion of competition between institutions and the structuring of a higher education market (Pritchard, 1994).

So how does the Investors in People process support the professional development of staff within the higher education market? In essence, an institution that is an Investor in People will:

- plan ahead and have clear measurable objectives that are continually monitored and updated;
- be clear what skills and knowledge are needed to achieve its goals and targets and to deliver the strategic plan;
- have identified what skills and knowledge all staff already have;
- plan and take action to fill any gaps between the skills and knowledge already held and those needed;
- look back after the action has been taken to see what impact the action has had on the business, if the action was effective in filling the gap and, if not, take further action.

(Adapted from Taylor and Thackwray, 1995, 1996)

The higher education sector meets all these criteria in abundance when applied to a variety of teaching, learning and research-related activities, less so when they are applied to the continuing professional development of its staff, especially those staff who are not directly involved in teaching and/or research.

To explore this more fully in a higher education context and with special emphasis on support staff, I will now examine the requirements relating to achieving the standard using the 23 indicators as the starting point.

1 Commitment

1.1 The commitment from top management to train and develop employees is communicated effectively throughout the organization

This is the cornerstone of the standard. The commitment must come from the Vice Chancellor and other senior staff and it must be believed by employees. It must apply equally to all staff in the institution – including cleaners and part-time staff at all levels and in all categories. Assessors may look for written evidence of commitment such as policy statements. They may ask how senior managers put this commitment over. Taking a broad sample of colleagues, ensuring the sample contains appropriate representation from men, women, ethnic minorities, part-time staff, new and mature colleagues and disabled employees is one way to ascertain just how senior managers' commitment is seen.

1.2 Employees at all levels are aware of the broad aims or vision of the organization

How and in what way have senior managers explained in broad terms what they, and therefore the institution, are trying to achieve? Higher Educational Institutions (HEIs) will also have to demonstrate how all employees contribute to these goals. For senior staff this may well mean demonstrating a good understanding of goals, targets and plans. For others this awareness could be demonstrated by relating what they and their department contribute to the organization. How does a research unit within a faculty contribute? What do estates staff believe their role to be in relation to the whole institution? How does the success or retention of individual students relate to organizational goals and what part do the caterers or the porters play? Assessors may look for written evidence in the form of departmental or team briefing notes. For example, research will be high on the corporate agenda; how and in what way are colleagues, especially those who are not directly involved, made aware of this?

1.3 The employer has considered what employees at all levels will contribute to the success of the organization, and has communicated this effectively to them

Everyone should know how what they do contributes to the success of the HEI. Rather than focus on narrow departmental or faculty interests colleagues should be aware of how they enhance the quality of the student experience and research. The assessor may ask staff if they know what they are expected to achieve, and how what they do contributes to the development of their department or faculty and the institution as a whole.

1.4 Where representative structures exist, communication takes place between management and representatives on the vision of where the organization is going and the contribution that employees (and their representatives) will make to its success

These representative structures include professional associations, trade unions and other local groups such as staff associations where they have a representative function. Evidence includes the minutes of meetings and other evidence of communication with representatives. Senior staff may well be asked what they have communicated to representatives. This will be checked against the response given by those representatives on what they have been told about where the HEI is going and what their role is in support of this.

NB: If the institution or autonomous unit has no 'representative structure', this indicator does not apply.

2 Planning

2.1 A written but flexible plan sets out the organization's goals and targets

Longer-term vision will be underpinned by clear goals or objectives for the HEI and a plan for achieving these which includes targets and short-term milestones. The assessor will expect to have evidence that there is a plan and not just a budget and that this plan is reviewed at least annually.

The strategic plan should be flexible and subject to review and updating as appropriate. It is not necessary for this plan to be in the form of just one document. Evidence of 'people planning' will be sought, local staff development plans being a good example. The assessor may well focus on future skill needs and how they are to be met. Here and throughout the standard there is no requirement to conform to a particular type of terminology. 'Aims and objectives', for example, is equally acceptable. The language used does not matter as long as the requirements of the standard are met.

2.2 A written plan identifies the organization's training and development needs, and specifies what action will be taken to meet these needs

The HEI will have planned the broad actions that will need to have been taken to meet the development needs. Clear links must be made between institutional objectives, training and development needs and action taken to meet those needs. A good example here is Information Technology (IT) training and development in support of new or upgraded technology. For example, if use of the Internet forms part of the student recruitment process, how will staff skill needs be met?

2.3 Training and development needs are regularly reviewed against goals and targets at the organization, team and individual level

If the HEI's direction changes or evolves, perhaps as a result of funding changes or a research assessment exercise, the consequences for broad training and development should be reviewed. Evidence of some form of informal or formal discussion on the reviewing of individual and team needs – at several levels – will be required and the evidence should demonstrate that this is an ongoing process. The assessor will expect managers to describe how they make the link between the strategic plan and objectives for training and development. Identifying and meeting the training and development needs of part-time staff and those with special needs may well be a focus here.

2.4 A written plan identifies the resources that will be used to meet training and development needs

These resources can be shown in the annual operating budget produced by all HEIs, rather than the more alien 'business plan'. The resources specified will be budget and staff allocated to development and training and who is responsible for it. A specific budget for the enhancement of research capability would be a good example. Note that this plan does not have to be the same plan as in 2.1 and 2.2, and it can be more than one document. Resources identified should be linked to the needs identified (see indicators 2.2, 2.3).

2.5 Responsibility for training and developing employees is clearly identified and understood throughout the organization, starting at the top

The draft version of this indicator did not include *'and understood'*. Someone at senior level should have overall responsibility for training and development. Entries in the UCoSDA Staff Development Contact Register 1996 often include Pro or Deputy Vice Chancellor with overall responsibility for staff development. Is this role widely understood internally?

Local departmental heads (and indeed anyone whose role includes the managing of people) should understand that they are responsible for developing the staff who report to them and what their role is. Evidence can be provided, for example, via job descriptions and policy statements. A sample of employees may be asked who is responsible for developing them. (In addition to themselves!)

2.6 Objectives are set for training and development actions at the organization, team and individual level

Objectives should be set for training and development actions before they occur. Actions may be identified to meet organizational, team or individual needs and objectives should be established at these levels as appropriate. An objective may be a quantifiable and measurable level of performance (eg publications) or a benchmark of achievement (eg results from audit and assessment). The assessor may look at training and development records to see if the expected outcomes are recorded. Employees at all levels may be asked if they were involved in agreeing the objectives before they undertook the development activity and what they were expected to be able to do as a result.

2.7 Where appropriate, training and development needs are linked to external standards such as National Vocational Qualifications (NVQs) or Scottish Vocational Qualifications (SVQs) and units

What is appropriate is up to the individual HEI, not any outside advising individual or agency. Demonstration of consideration of external standards will be expected by the assessor and it is worth noting that N/SVQs are a favoured training outcome within the Investors in People initiative generally. If N/SVQs are not used, an assessor may ask why not, and have other standards been used instead?

3 Action

3.1 All new employees are introduced effectively to the organization and all employees new to a job are given the training and development they need to do that job

This indicator covers both corporate and local induction processes and implicitly assumes their effective integration. People who change jobs within the organization should also be included. The assessor may look at examples of induction programmes for selected employees and ask a sample of new staff about their initial induction experiences. The opportunity to locate induction clearly as part of continuing professional development should not be missed. Effective induction contributes positive evidence towards indicators 1.2, 1.3, 2.3 and 3.6.

3.2 Managers are effective in carrying out their responsibilities for training and developing employees

Are managers effective in supporting and promoting training and development to the standards expected by the organization? It is up to the individual HEI to define what it means by effective, in much the same way that each individual institution defines what it means by quality for purposes of audit and assessment. Support for such initiatives as mentoring and related peer support activities for all staff will be reviewed. HEIs may wish to take the opportunity to include peer observation or support of teaching as evidence. The recent HEFCE report on quality assessment 1992–95 includes several examples of common characteristics of excellent education that can be included as elements within the overall action plan. For example 'clear commitment to good teaching, staff development that promotes good teaching and learning' sits well with this indicator.

Improving research and publications was a major objective for the college. A considerable amount of time and resources was being sunk into supporting the leap from being a largely teaching-oriented institution to somewhere with a credible research base. There were programmes offered on preparing to publish, how to supervise students, how to undertake research, research methods, and so on. A group of technicians, all graduates, were refused permission by their line managers to join any of these programmes in spite of their offer to give up their own time during the evening and at weekends.

The commitment may have been at the top – and with the technicians – but how can an institution 'police' its less able managers?

3.3 Managers are actively involved in supporting employees to meet their training and development needs

Are managers actively supporting individuals within the training and development culture of the organization? Assessors may look for involvement in coaching, evidence of briefing staff before training and development programmes and discussion of programme outcomes. Managers will be providing support so the new skills can be used as part of normal working practice (for example, following programmes on teaching more students, are the appropriate resources made available?). Managers will actively participate in the evaluation of training and development by monitoring performance. Evidence of performance being monitored by less formal structures such as peer observation can be offered.

The porter whose job it was to deliver the internal mail was always late and getting later. Without consultation, his manager sent him on a basic time management course. The departmental objective was to see that the mail arrived on time. Following the course his timing did not improve, it got worse. He was spotted by a senior member of staff taking a rubber band out of a large bag of rubber bands and tying it around a wheel of his trolley. When asked why he was doing this, he said that the wheel kept falling off when he went up and down stairs and he had been told by his manager that there was no money in the kitty to repair it . . .

What was the real training and development need and for whom?

3.4 All employees are made aware of the training and development opportunities open to them

Advice on training and development opportunities must be equally available to all employees. Employees are informed when new training and development opportunities become available. The assessor may check systems for informing employees of these opportunities probably via a sample of employees of varying ages and length of service.

3.5 All employees are encouraged to help identify and meet their job-related training and development needs

People are actively involved in identifying and discussing their own development needs within the organization's objectives. They should understand that they share responsibility for their development and are encouraged to develop themselves (long-standing custom and practice in academic departments but perhaps without the emphasis on the organization's objectives). Appropriate help and guidance should be available – including the provision of relevant academic, professional and trade journals. The assessor may look at development plans for a sample of employees and ask the employees if they believe they share responsibility for their own development. Have they been encouraged and helped? It is important to note that a narrow definition of 'job-related' is inappropriate. Investors in People guidance includes the following: 'Job-related means relevant to what individuals can contribute to the success of the organization'.

3.6 Action takes place to meet the training and development needs of individuals, teams and the organization

Check that the training and development identified actually happens, subject to the organization's own priorities and budget. Development should be seen in its broadest sense, for example incorporating mentoring, coaching, shadowing. The assessor may wish to follow through records for a sample of employees, from the identification of training needs to the training and development action. A sample of employees may be asked if what was agreed at, for example, appraisal, actually happened.

4 Evaluation

4.1 The organization evaluates the impact of training and development actions on knowledge, skills and attitude

Is there a system for evaluating if a particular training and development activity achieved the objectives set for it? (This should relate to indicator 2.6 where the objectives set for improving 'knowledge, skills and attitude' will be found.) The assessor may look for evidence of evaluation methods and will expect something beyond the level of the 'happy sheet', such as targeted follow-up questionnaires, interviews, discussions with participants and their managers or even testing in some instances. How were outcomes of particular activities followed up? The method used for evaluating this 'learning' (ie the impact of 'training and development actions') is up to the HEI.

4.2 The organization evaluates the impact of training and development actions on performance

Check that the training and development needs of the organization, the team and the individual have been met. (See indicator 2.4.) A programme may have met its objectives but has it made a difference? For example, if a course on improving supervisory skills is deemed successful because the participants enjoyed it, the managers approved of it and it is in line with corporate objectives, how does the institution know that the skills are being applied? The assessor may look for evidence of evaluation against the training and development plans of the organization, team and individual. NVQs could be a useful example here, providing the link is made between objective, training and development and performance improvement. How does the institution evaluate whether the desired outcome of meeting that training and development need is achieved? Again, the system for evaluating the impact of training and development on performance is up to the organization, but should be based on the objectives set by indicator 2.6.

4.3 The organization evaluates the contribution of training and development to the achievement of its goals and targets

This indicator makes the link between 'the improvements in performance resulting from training and development actions'. Were the organization's goals and targets met? Was performance improved and was the return on training and development realized? In what way do the results offer opportunities to further refine and develop organizational objectives? The assessor may look for evidence that the senior management or the senior decision-making bodies (such as senates, councils, academic boards, governing bodies) have reviewed the contribution of the training and development activity and taken action as a result. Locally, the assessor may wish to discuss how training and development activity is reviewed at team level. The institution will need to link its evaluation of the overall impact of training and development activities to indicator 2.2. Appraisal offers a useful example – as a result of the training for appraisal has the institution been more effective in achieving its objectives?

The university had recently introduced an appraisal scheme. After some considerable debate it was agreed that the same system should be applied to all staff in the same way, given the institution's commitment to equality of opportunity. The system was very much paper-based, and relied on staff to fill in a pre-interview form, discuss it and then use this as a basis for the full appraisal interview. The report was written up by the manager and signed by both parties before being sent on to personnel.

Several groups of staff, notably those whose job did not entail a considerable amount of writing and talking, were concerned by this and it was clear that they were disadvantaged by the system. A more flexible system allowed for a pre-discussion, without forms, and a full appraisal meeting, again without forms, to take place. It was the line manager's responsibility to take notes and use them as a basis for the production of a short report in draft for the employee to read, agree and sign accordingly. This proved far more successful and allayed most of the fears of these particular groups of staff.

4.4 Top management understands the broad costs and benefits of training and developing employees

This does not mean that everything is quantified in money terms, but there should be an attempt to measure costs in broad terms and value the benefits and to plan ahead on the basis of this information. The assessor will expect to discuss this with senior staff. The assessor may also test this out by discussing the understanding of the costs and benefits of training and development and how these lead to making judgements about future developmental activity. The HEFCE report on quality assessment notes that one area where room for improvement was identified is the 'quality of academic management' and 'their effectiveness in communicating and developing good practice.' In essence, can – and do – key staff ask and answer these questions: 'Was our overall commitment to training and development worthwhile?' and 'How do you know?'

4.5 Action takes place to implement improvements to training and development identified as a result of evaluation

The organization should take action as a result of evaluation to improve those areas of its training and development activities where a need arises. This can apply equally to a programme (eg the introduction of IT training for curriculum development) or a system (eg where the appraisal system requires improvement). The assessor may follow through a sample of organizational, team and individual evaluations to see if the action points are fed into the next plan and acted upon. Has last year's evaluation made a difference? Clearly the process is ongoing and underpins the commitment to continuous improvement. The guidance notes for this indicator advise that 'this indicator should not lengthen the time required for an organization to generate sufficient evidence for its first assessment' . . . 'however, at reassessment, all organizations will have had sufficient time to implement actions following an overall evaluation and will need to show evidence of this'.

4.6 Top management's continuing commitment to training and developing employees is demonstrated to all employees

Everyone should be told how training and development have contributed to the organization's performance and publicity should be given to training and development achievements. This indicator is linked to 1.1 and emphasizes the fact that the actions of senior management should be perceived by employees to indicate a long-term commitment to developing people. This indicator will be particularly pertinent at the time of reassessment. Useful evidence here includes the recording, awareness or even celebration of training and development achievements. As a sector we perhaps have more experience of this with regard to academic achievements in research and publications, and need to broaden this to embrace all staff. Of particular import to higher education at the moment is the expectation that evident commitment to training and development should continue through difficult times. (Or, as the guidance puts it, 'adverse trading conditions'.)

Some key messages

It is difficult to disagree with the principles underpinning the standard. This does not, of course, mean that actually going for recognition as an Investor in People is universally regarded as a good thing. On the contrary, some colleagues working in higher education have expressed strong views as to why they feel it is inappropriate for them and their institutions. Often this is to do with the 'language' of investors which until the 1995/6 review of the standard was oriented overmuch towards business and manufacturing.

It is increasingly accepted that the single most important factor differentiating one organization from another is the skills, knowledge and expertise of its people (Taylor and Thackwray, 1995). This is, perhaps, especially true of universities and colleges. Most have access to similar ranges of equipment, technology and other facilities. Therefore, it is how well these are used that makes the difference. The sector relies considerably on the skills and attitudes of people to demonstrate commitment to the efficient delivery of a quality service. That notwithstanding, many universities and colleges do not consider training and development of people an investment. They still see it as a cost. Institutional and departmental staff development is, as a consequence, often not planned strategically nor is it clearly linked to corporate objectives. It is, in many universities, clearly not equally available to all employees. Programmes and other developmental activities are rarely evaluated at the point of delivery, let alone later in terms of their impact on the enhanced effectiveness of working practices.

It has to be hoped that the development of clear objectives for the institution, faculty and department and making these objectives relevant to all staff – academic or porter, librarian or cook – will engender that essential sense of ownership via an understanding of what needs to be achieved and what every individual's contribution is (Thackwray, 1994).

References

Chambers, J (1996) 'Does this mean the gardener has to read the strategic plan?', title of keynote presentation at the UCoSDA National Investors in People in Higher Education Network and Forum meeting, University of Warwick.

HEQC/UCoSDA (1995, 1996) *Investors in People in Higher Education Network Directory*, HEQC/UCoSDA, London and Sheffield.

Pritchard, RMO (1994) 'Government power in British higher education, *Studies in Higher Education*, vol. 19, no. 3, pp. 253, 265.

Taylor, P and Thackwray, R (1995) *Investors in People Explained*, Kogan Page, London.

Taylor, P and Thackwray, R (1996) *Investors in People Explained*, revised second edition, Kogan Page, London.

Thackwray, R (1994) 'University staff: a worthwhile investment?', in *University-wide Change, Staff and Curriculum Development*, SEDA, Birmingham.

Training Agency (1987) *Training in Britain* 1987, Employment Department, Sheffield.

—— 10 ——

Developing managers: towards management learning

George Gordon and Robin Middlehurst

Introduction

Learning, development, change . . . these are the buzz words of the 1990s. Yet what do they mean for managers in universities and colleges, for those who are 'in charge' of development and training and for others at different levels of the institution? This chapter tackles these questions by looking at the context of change in higher education and the consequences for the roles of managers, explores parallel changes in the world of management development and seeks to explain why management learning is important. These issues form the conceptual background to the practical examples and suggestions contained in the second part of the chapter. In this second part, some examples of existing practice are described and some ideas for the future presented.

Changing contexts

The Higher Education (HE) environment

Higher education in Britain is going through a process of fundamental change, in that it is now making a decisive transition from an elite to a mass system, at the same time as relationships between the state and the public services are being radically reappraised throughout the western world. What we are observing in our study [of Britain, Sweden and Norway] is institutional leaders responding to the insinuation of new values: performance, efficiency, competition in the emerging markets.

(Henkel, 1997)

Those managers and organisations that see themselves as helpless in the face of internal or external pressure soon lose faith in their ability to affect events positively.

(Cannon, 1996)

Discussions at the regional workshops touched on two further aspects of managing change in higher education:

(i) the perception, within the sector, of rapid change and a high level of fluidity in policy initiatives;
(ii) external perceptions that higher education has changed little and is unresponsive to calls for change.

(Middlehurst *et al.*, 1995)

These quotations from recent studies of higher education and its wider environment offer an initial view of the context for management in the UK in the late 1990s. For universities, change may be viewed in different ways. For many, their perspectives will inevitably be coloured by history since universities are amongst the small group of organizations that have been in existence for many centuries. That longevity may hint at considerable stability, constancy of purpose, even of enduring centrality to societies, but successful survival has involved negotiating substantial political, religious and economic changes and important diversification of the constancy of purpose, notably with the emerging ethos of the Germanic research university and the acceptance of preparation of individuals for various professions (eg, religion, law, medicine, veterinary science, engineering, dentistry).

Evolutionary, and occasionally radical, changes, have affected institutions and systems of higher education throughout history. What may be different at present is the scale, nature, locus and pace of those changes. In fifty years' time when students of higher education reflect upon the last quarter of the twentieth century, they may come to different conclusions about the amount and consequences of change from those written by current observers and commentators. Generally, the prevailing thrust is that change is rapid and substantial and significantly influenced by external forces and pressures. Whether these are predominantly catalytic in character or the underlying cause of change is another matter.

Breathtaking is a commonly heard description of the pace of activity in higher education today. Activity is not necessarily equated directly to effectiveness but it is closely associated to workload. That may explain the levels of stress and frustration within the system. It is not too fanciful to assert that internal and external stakeholders share a common desire for increased effectiveness, although they may diverge significantly in detailed interpretations of the implications for strategies, policies, practices, processes and outcomes.

A great deal of change can affect a system and individual institutions in a comparatively short period of time. In British higher education the changes post-1985 include: the introduction of periodic research assessments; external quality audits and assessment of teaching provision; the abolition of the binary divide; the creation of unified funding councils; massive growth in student enrolments; shifts in the sources of institutional funding; mergers and associations between previously independent institutions; and a wide commitment to faculty and staff development.

(Gordon, 1995)

Looking towards the new century, the Committee of Vice Chancellors and Principals (1995) identified four key influences upon the future shape of higher education, namely, the need and demand for lifelong learning; the requirements of learners for alternative types and modes of provision; the impact of new technology; and the changing boundaries between higher education and other sectors of education and business. These items, along with issues relating to the standards of educational provision, increased research selectivity, the funding of students, the steering and governance of the system and of institutions, and the systematic preparation and continuing development of staff have featured prominently in the evidence presented to, and investigated by, the National Inquiry into Higher Education (the Dearing Review).

Governance and management

In Britain, massive growth in student numbers has not been matched by growth in funding. In essence, institutions have been expected to increase volumes of output at a lessening unit cost without diminution of quality. Perhaps as a consequence, expectations of external accountability for the use of public moneys has mushroomed. The use of the moneys remains vested with the management of the institutions. For the new universities and colleges which were previously under local government or direct central government control, senior management has, at least apparently, acquired increased control over the use of funds. In reality, the degree of discretion is circumscribed by mounting controls over financial practice and the reducing leeway that most institutions have as virtually every source of funding is squeezed. In summary, British higher education from the mid-1980s to the mid-1990s underwent expansion and diversification against a backcloth of pressures for economy, efficiency and accountability and of changes in various sets of relationships: with government; with buffer bodies such as the Funding Councils and Research Councils; with employers and professional organizations; and with students. Many institutions have a substantial proportion of adult learners, often studying part-time and at least partly off-campus, and they have as a result sought to make their provision as flexible as possible. In contrast, there are institutions that are almost exclusively traditional in the sense that the vast majority of undergraduate students are under 21 years of age at point of entry, are reading for an Honours degree by full-time study and spend at least one year of their course in a university hall of residence or college.

Looking to the next decade Harvey (1996) anticipates the emergence of a genuine mass system where the modes and methods of instruction and support will have altered in order to smooth transitions for students, facilitate learning, emphasize attainment and quality, assure standards, be more open, transparent and responsive to students and offer continuous education in institutions, workplaces, homes and anywhere that offers telecommunication access. Lest Harvey be considered too futuristic, Levine (1993) in a study of the expectations of undergraduates at 30 American campuses, concluded that students wanted convenient access, polite and efficient treatment and high-quality products at a low cost.

Inevitably, changes have not impacted evenly within the system. Indeed, research selectivity, by definition, is intended to differentiate. Other changes, such as supernetworks, are enabling devices that offer opportunities, although the full potential may be impaired if competition reigns supreme. After at least two decades where inter-institutional competition was encouraged, switching the focus to inter-institutional and wider collaboration is proving to be difficult.

Even in the much changed framework of British higher education the depiction of the American college or university as a prototypic organized anarchy (Cohen and March, 1974) retains some validity. Indeed, the management literature has shifted in emphasis towards the potential benefits of flatter, devolved management of professionals. As a former vice-chancellor who has returned to the primary role of research professor, Johnston is well placed to comment on this complex situation. He describes the modern university as a catallaxy.

> Management is an imperfect science – but some management is a more imperfect science than others. University management falls close to the more imperfect pole, because the institutional goals – high quality research and teaching, sustained by efficient and effective administration – are not conducive to critical path analysis which characterises the operational environment of a Hayekian economy. Management is crucially involved in the resource allocation process but that is insufficient in itself; it must be associated with stimulating leadership, a supportive collegial ethos and a great deal of serendipity. In a nutshell, it is paramount to appoint excellent people, give them good working conditions, make clear what your (realistic) expectations are, sustain them through the bad times, celebrate with them during the good and hope for the best.
>
> (Johnston, 1996)

Senior managers therefore, must exercise prudent stewardship, use resources wisely, offer sensitive and supportive leadership, recognize and address the things that motivate staff and students, be supported and advised by excellent people, take some calculated risks and be blessed with a measure of good fortune.

Attempts to describe and evaluate these managerial issues are rendered increasingly difficult by the sheer complexities of the British system of higher education in detailed matters of governance, organization and management. Institutions of higher education range in scale from small colleges to complex federations spanning several campuses. The largest institutions are major businesses. They employ thousands of people and have annual turnovers in excess of £100 million. Often they are one of the largest employers in the local region, yet almost every institution of higher education in Britain now has agreements with institutions, agencies, governments and other bodies overseas. Large institutions operate numerous financial and contractual arrangements. Increasingly large sums of money must be borrowed to develop residences and to construct new buildings for the core activities of teaching and research. All of the endeavours require planning and monitoring. To perform effectively institutions have developed new areas of administrative expertise, of intrapreneurship and entrepreneurship, planning, evaluating and monitoring.

Part of the changing context has involved devolution of responsibilities, financial and academic, from central bodies within institutions to faculties or schools or departments or cost centres and to those responsible for managing, leading and monitoring programmes and services. In some measure these structural changes can be viewed as moving towards layered models, but not top-down hierarchies.

Organizational cultures

To complete this review of the changing context of UK higher education, brief reference should be made to three models of the cultures and organizational frameworks of higher education. First, Bergquist (1992) has written of the four cultures of the academy: collegial; managerial; negotiating and developmental. Second, McNay (1993) used the dimensions of policy definition and operational control to produce the quartet of collegium, bureaucracy, corporation and enterprise. Thorpe and Cuthbert (1996) offered the quartet of autonomous professional, professional market, managerial market and market bureaucracy as a means of categorizing institutions of higher education in the late 1990s. Institutions classed as autonomous professional are leaders in research. Their prestige limits the influence of external bodies such as government. Professors continue to exercise considerable influence.

By contrast, in institutions classified as professional market, the balance of power shifts to management in order to deal with their greater potential exposure to market risk. In this case students gain and Professors lose some influence. Managerial market institutions do not have the independence of autonomous professional institutions but seek to pursue the dual mission of research and teaching. Thorpe and Cuthbert conclude that, in these institutions, managerial influence has increased, as has happened in the institutions most exposed to market forces, the market bureaucracies, where research is a minor component of the overall portfolio of activities. Student recruitment and retention are vital for those institutions. Thorpe and Cuthbert argue that professional market and managerial market institutions are converging whilst the autonomous professional and market bureaucratic types are diverging. The latter situation represents the separation of the small cluster of leading research universities from those institutions which receive virtually no funding for research from any source. The dynamic battleground in terms of institutional management and positioning is focusing at present upon the professional market and managerial market types of institutions as they endeavour to maintain a credible foothold in research whilst seeking to strengthen or develop reputations as centres of excellence for teaching and consultancy.

Changing managerial roles

Heads of department

Moses and Roe (1990) draw attention to the fact that departmental struct-ures have been a feature of British universities for about a century and for much of that time departments were led by the sole professor who combined the dual tasks of academic leader with that of administrator or manager. With the emergence of multi-professorial departments, the rotational pattern of headship was gradually adopted. In pre-1992 universities, that practice is now commonplace, with members of the department being consulted about suitable successors, although the ultimate decision does not rest with the department. In the post-1992 universities and in the colleges, academic managers are appointed, often after a formal process of advertisement and interview, either to fixed con-tracts (often of five or seven years) or to permanent posts.

Nowadays, whatever the type of institution, heads will normally receive a contract which outlines their principal duties and responsibilities. Some institutions openly list these in publications such as management or staff handbooks. The conclusions from an American study (Baldridge et al., 1978) about the nature of universities continue to have some relevance for managerial roles. Baldridge et al. concluded that management in universities had to deal with six important contextual characteristics, namely, goal ambiguity, professional staff, the autonomy of sub-units, part-time decision-makers, environmental vulnerability and undifferentiated functions (ie, lecturers do not necessarily perform a fundamentally different function from professors).

Watson (1986) formulated five roles for heads of department: intellectual leader, co-ordinator/administrator, representative, resource mobilizer, personnel administrator. In their Australian study, Moses and Roe (1990) found that the heads they interviewed attached greatest importance (in descending order) to: selecting staff; maintaining morale; developing long-range plans; implementing long-range plans; stimulating research and publications; serving as an advocate for the department; evaluating the performance of staff; supporting staff subjected to unfair treatment or criticism; encouraging good teaching; and encouraging high performance. Heads disliked (again in descending order of importance): dealing with unsatisfactory performance; timetabling classes; supervising departmental examination procedures; processing departmental correspondence; participating in university committees; organizing research grants for themselves; seeking outside funding; addressing conflict; and evaluating performance for promotion and tenure.

Interestingly, in a recent study of a sample of department heads in America and Australia, Sarros, Gmelch and Tanewski (1997), found that the overall level of stress was moderate. It was higher for female heads and for heads aged 30–39 and lowest for heads over 60 years of age. On average external appointees had a higher level of job satisfaction than internal appointees. Differences also occurred in terms of age, with those in the 30–39 and 60+ categories having the highest levels of job satisfaction. Associate Professors were the most dissatisfied with workload and the pace of work. Levels of satisfaction also varied by length of appointment to the post, with the middle group, 6–10 years' experience, being the most dissatisfied. The authors found that becoming a head had an impact upon maintaining a record of publication. Overall, Australian departmental heads and American departmental chairs displayed similar profiles on a number of dimensions of the role. The top five stressors were: 'having insufficient time to stay current in my field'; 'attending meetings which take up too much time'; 'feeling I have too heavy a work load'; 'trying to gain financial support for department programmes'; and 'meeting report and other paper-work deadlines'. The authors concluded that heads recognize that the job will be complex, demanding and busy. It appears that the greatest tension surrounds the desire to maintain active scholarship and achieve personal development with the partial sacrifice of self in the interest of the departments. Sarros et al. suggest that the impact is not restricted to heads and chairs and that academics at middle levels and below might benefit from more mentoring in order to develop their records in research and publication. One could add that other facets of the role of an academic might also be nurtured by appropriate coaching and mentoring.

In a review of the efficiency of management of British universities, Jarratt (1985) stressed the importance of effective management of departments, which were perceived as the fundamental organizational units. Somewhat controversially, Jarratt suggested that if a choice had to be made between an effective manager and an academic leader, the balance should tip in favour of the former. By implication, the arguments of Sarros et al. (1997), Gmelch et al. (1996) and others, indicate that active scholarship is perceived by heads and their peers as an essential prerequisite if the head or chair is to have credibility amongst peers, or to be accepted as a model.

Wider management roles

In most institutions, while academic departments are the main organizational units, management cannot be equated solely with heading those areas. Often there will be a myriad of other academic centres, administrative and support areas and, within every unit or centre, management tasks of varying scale and complexity are performed by a host of individuals. Moreover, some of these will span wide areas of the institution and, indeed, involve relationships with external bodies and other institutions.

For every activity undertaken by the institution (eg, teaching, research, consultancy, student affairs, external relations, finance, personnel, health and safety, information technology, academic and technical support facilities, commercial development, residences and catering, estates management, international relations, alumni relations, fund-raising, staff development), managers exercise responsibility for tasks, resources and the implementation of policies and codes of practice.

The range and diversity are considerable. New roles emerge from time to time, or more commonly the way of managing an area or issue is reviewed and new structural arrangements are implemented. Additionally, some functions gain greater prominence. An example of the latter is the work on the employment, career management and development of contract research staff which has been stimulated by the *Concordat on Contract Research Staff Career Management* (CVCP *et al.*, 1996).

Structural change can be illustrated by the adoption of matrix arrangements where, for example, courses are managed by course leaders who draw staff from a number of departments. Not only does that raise issues about management and leadership development of course leaders (Wisker, 1996) but it presents potential tensions between sets of managers, course leaders and heads of department, where the latter are normally responsible for the performance of staff and the allocation of duties and the former are responsible for the provision and staffing of courses. Decentralization of administrative, financial or computing staff can pose similar problems of dual reporting lines. Another example of potential tension surrounds the expectation that heads of department exercise managerial responsibility for all staff in the department and the tradition that principal research investigators have a considerable degree of sovereignty over the management of the researchers employed to work on projects for which they are responsible. None of these challenges are new but they have altered in detailed impact because of developments in accountability and the passing of additional pieces of legislation.

In varying degree three bundles of activities feature prominently in managerial roles:

- information handling, gathering and dissemination;
- procedures, criteria, systems and co-ordination;
- design, direction and navigation.

Accountability and other external pressures may appear to generate greater demands for the first two sets of roles, yet all of them are necessary and, in fact, often interconnected. Again, the pressures of accountability, the demands of legislation, the strains on resources, the need for carefully calculated risk-taking, logically favour a greater emphasis upon analysis, evidencing and justification. Yet Rosemary Stewart (1997) provides a timely reminder that the days of managers are often chaotic, that managers do their jobs differently partly because of different perceptions of the role, that they have different strengths and weaknesses, and that managing is more a human activity than a logical, analytical, ordered process. Clearly, the management task is complex and demanding; preparation and support for the role will therefore need to be conceived creatively and provided in a variety of ways to suit different needs and situations.

Trends in management development: towards management and organizational learning

This section concentrates first on relationships between management thought and management development outside the universities and colleges, before commenting on trends inside the higher education system.

Management development outside higher education

The story of how managers prepare for, are inducted into, and improve their knowledge, skill and understanding about their management roles and tasks has changed over time. Management itself has altered through changes in ways of working (eg, from full, permanent employment to part-time, short-term contracts), changes in the nature of business, including an increased customer orientation and emphasis on 'collaboration to compete', and shifts in the economic, social and political environment of organizations. Management development has been similarly affected. Changes in emphasis and orientation can be observed by monitoring changes in language: a movement from management 'training' to management 'education and development', from management 'development' towards management 'learning', and so to concepts of 'organizational learning'.

Trends in management development also reflect shifts in theories about the nature of management and managerial work. Early twentieth-century thinking, influenced by the work of Taylor (1911) and Fayol (1916) was both strongly rationalist and essentially task-oriented; by mid-century, for example through the work of McGregor (1960) and through the series of Michigan and Ohio leadership studies of the 1940s and 1950s (Stodgill and Coons, 1957), the 'human side of enterprise' had entered the picture. The combining of these two streams of thought led to the development of a much more complex picture of management in which tasks and relationships were intertwined and often in tension with each other.

Flowing from a deeper understanding of management interactions and transactions, there emerged studies of managerial roles (Mintzberg, 1973), of management styles (Blake and Mouton, 1964; Hersey and Blanchard, 1977) and subsequently of the human and symbolic context of organizations through the medium of 'culture' (Harrison, 1972; Handy, 1979; Deal and Kennedy, 1982), extended through studies of the attributes of 'excellence' in successful companies (Peters and Waterman, 1982). The identification of managers and management with organizational effectiveness had reached an important juncture.

The 1980s and 1990s have seen a fusion of ideas about the management task and its context, thus providing new perspectives. Systems thinking, emerging from operational research (Checkland, 1981), has focused particularly on interactions and transactions within and between organizations or other 'systems', providing insights into management and organizational 'processes' – a departure from tasks or interpersonal relations. A focus on business processes has illuminated the ways in which information, communication and influence either flow or are blocked in transactional relationships. In parallel, the 'quality movement', initiated by Deming (1982), Juran (1988) and Crosby (1984), has acted as a catalyst for other changes in management practice by combining emphases on tasks and business imperatives, internal and external relationships, communication and information flows and the use of data for problem-solving. What has emerged is a philosophy and an approach to organizational design and development which are driven both by the changing needs of customers, clients and stakeholders and by a competitive requirement for 'continuous improvement'. Variations on both of these themes – systems thinking and quality – are still being played out in a variety of ways (Senge, 1990), most recently in concepts of the learning organization (for discussions in the context of HE see Duke, 1992; Schuller, 1995).

In the context of developing managers, connections between thinking about management and organizations and thinking about development can be made. Management training reflects a notion of management as a set of technical tasks for which managers can be prepared through systematic instruction and practice. In contrast, notions of management education and development suggest that the practice of management is neither clear-cut nor capable of being reduced to a series of uncontroversial techniques. It is, instead, essentially contingent, dependent on the situation, the task in hand, the operative time scale, the culture and the people involved. What are required therefore in developmental terms are means of raising awareness about the nature of the task or role from a variety of perspectives, as well as approaches which encourage managers to engage in reflecting and improving on their performance in a managerial role continuously and progressively in the course of their careers.

The shift from management 'development' to 'management learning' is more subtle, reflecting a concern about ownership and engagement in the process by managers themselves: development is directed at you; learning is something that you do and achieve yourself. In practice, this shift in emphasis has had important consequences for the way in which management development or learning is organized and conceived, for example, as separate from the day-to-day task of management by the provision of opportunities for structured reflection, or as an important part of the ongoing task of management as a means of improving performance, understanding and diagnosis. Linking management and organizational learning reflects a growing appreciation of the role of management, not just in contributing to current performance, but also in developing organizations for future success, a role which requires leadership (Kotter, 1990). An emphasis on organizational learning is much broader in scope than earlier notions of development since learning can take place in a variety of contexts, through a variety of media, in informal as well as formal ways, at different times and stages of a career and through engagement with a range of (management or organizational) tasks, processes and experiences. The nature of such learning at the individual level is captured vividly in *The Lessons of Experience* (McCall *et al.*, 1988) which describes the learning achieved at different phases and through crucial experiences of managerial life. More recently, at least one management consultancy has developed a diagnostic profile based on these critical lessons of experience. The profile provides feedback to individuals on their current strengths and management learning needs (Andrews Munro, 1996).

Burgoyne (1988) offered a model which reflects how organizations have approached management development over time; later this model was refined further with colleagues, towards the notion of 'The Learning Company' (Pedler *et al.*, 1991). The early model of 'Levels of Maturity of Organizational Management Development' is in the form of a ladder with stage 1 representing the lowest rung:

Stage 1: No systematic management development

No systematic or deliberate management development – total reliance on *laissez-faire*, uncontrived processes of 'development'.

Stage 2: Isolated, tactical management development

Isolated and *ad hoc* tactical management development activities are established in response to local problems, crises or sporadically identified general problems.

Stage 3: Integrated and co-ordinated structural and developmental tactics

In those areas which impinge directly on the individual manager, ie assisting learning and career structure management, management development tactics are integrated and co-ordinated.

Stage 4: A management development strategy to implement corporate policy

A management development strategy plays its part in implementing corporate policies through human resource planning, providing a strategic framework and direction for career structure management and of learning, education and training.

Stage 5: Management development as input to corporate policy formation

Management development processes feed information into corporate decision-making processes on the organization's managerial assets, strengths, weakness and potential, and contribute to the forecasting and analysis of the manageability of proposed projects, ventures, changes.

Stage 6: Strategic development of the management of corporate policy

Management development processes enhance the nature and quality of corporate policy forming processes which they also inform and help implement.

By stage 6, it is only a small leap towards the idea that management learning can enhance the quality of corporate policy formation and, beyond this, to notions of corporate policy formation being a learning process. As Pedler, Burgoyne and Boydell describe it:

> company policy and strategy formation, together with implementation, evaluation and improvement, are consciously structured as a learning process . . . Managerial acts are thus conscious experiments, rather than set solutions. Deliberate small-scale experiments and feed-back loops are built into the planning process to enable continuous improvement in the light of experience.
>
> (Pedler, Burgoyne and Boydell, 1991)

Management development inside the higher education sector

In a public lecture in 1987, Burgoyne, commenting on the Management Charter Initiative in the UK (which was designed to improve the education and training of managers), noted that the focus was too much on the individual manager and the organizational systems dedicated to his (or occasionally her) development, and too little on management development for the organization as a whole. Ten years later, this comment provides a fairly accurate picture of the majority of management development activity in UK HE. In some cases, even this picture is too advanced. In practice, however, the logical sequencing of a staged model may not operate and elements of a later 'advanced' stage may exist on a prevailing bedrock of early stages. Thus, in many cases Burgoyne's Stages 1 or 2 above, 'no systematic', or 'isolated tactical management development' probably remain the order of the day. There are, of course, many reasons underlying this position, for example, perceptions of management and of training or development in universities (see Middlehurst, 1993), questions of resources and resource priorities, the nature of academic organizations, and in some cases, the form of what is provided as 'development' for managers. Whatever the cause of this situation, some other countries, notably North America and Australia, with established conferences for departmental heads or chairs and programmes for senior managers, appear to have been more pro-active than the UK. That said, national, regional and institutional programmes do exist in the UK and are being strengthened.

Two surveys of management development – Brown and Atkins in 1986 for the Committee of Vice Chancellors and Principals (CVCP), and Partington *et al.* (1994) for the Universities' and Colleges' Staff Development Agency (UCoSDA) – illustrate upward trends in the quantity of activity taking place in the UK, but they do not reveal extensive changes in the orientation, form, purposes or underlying conceptions of this 'provision'. There are only a few universities that have consciously and systematically implemented a shift from management to organizational development and still fewer that have clearly made the move from development to learning in individual or organizational terms. However, several developments, notably the growth of institutions seeking Investors in People status (accreditation for a corporate approach to training, development and evaluation of performance and potential) and the rise of different forms of external evaluations of quality (Quality Audit, Quality Assessment of Teaching, BS5750 Quality Systems), are now having an impact on the ways in which management development – and more broadly, staff development – is linked to improvement and change in the institution as a whole.

Why is management learning important?

Noting the emphasis placed on management development and management learning outside higher education (particularly, but not exclusively, in parts of the private sector) provides a benchmark against which to measure the perceived importance of both of these inside HE. Why is management learning apparently seen as of greater importance outside HE, but not inside it? The answer, we would suggest, lies in different traditions of management and differing perceptions about the value of management learning.

In the private sector, and increasingly in many parts of the public sector (Pollitt, 1990; 1995), the role of management has been seen as pivotal to the effectiveness of organizations, particularly in the context of resource deployment and resource control which lead to the successful delivery of products and services that satisfy customers or clients. In contrast, in the field of professional services (or performing arts) much greater emphasis tends to be placed on the competence, skill and overall quality of practitioners than on the skills of managers and management, despite the fact that many practitioners combine both roles. This contrast may have arisen out of differences in the nature of professional activities: in the private, business sector, the organization of work has tended to develop around groups or teams and larger organizational units while professional organizations have grown out of loose constellations of individual contributors. The task of co-ordination and integration of services and performance in professional service organizations has therefore been seen as one of facilitation and support for 'the main game' which takes place on stage or in the front-line. These different traditions are now changing, but the cultures and mind-sets that have developed around them are still strong, certainly at the levels of rhetoric and preferred language.

Views on the value of development and learning also appear to differ. While parts of the private and public sectors in the UK appear, to varying degrees, to have made the transition to regarding individual and corporate learning as an investment that directly affects competitiveness and the bottom line, most HE institutions still view development as a cost and an activity which is not obviously or systematically related to strategic planning, institutional survival and development. The perception persists among some senior practitioners or managers in universities and colleges that development is for others, although training in quick tips and techniques can be useful at the point at which management roles have to be taken on (Middlehurst, 1993).

The combination of external and internal forces impacting upon institutions of higher education is clearly highlighting the importance of effective management. However, to convince those who work in higher education that management and organizational learning are also important, it may be necessary to look seriously at how management and management development are currently conceived and 'delivered' in higher education, against a background of how professionals approach the task of learning. As a first step in this self-examination, a number of examples are presented of ways in which management development, in the broadest sense, is currently approached in UK higher education.

Strategies in use: approaches to management learning and organizational development

In this section, management development is taken to include formal activities, mounted by universities and colleges, or their agents, that are designed to further the knowledge, understanding, experiences and ability of managers to carry out and improve their roles and duties. The first two programmes, one in England and one in Scotland, are essentially course-based, aimed at the development of individuals and achieved by taking managers away from their day-to-day routine and mixing participants from different institutions; the third is a group-based approach aimed at ongoing managerial learning; the fourth is an institution-based development; and the fifth example offers some perspectives on approaches to management and organizational learning from a sector-wide programme.

Management development for individuals: the COSHEP Management Programme

The two-part programme mounted on behalf of the COSHEP Staff Development Committee has operated since the early 1990s. It is open to nominations from all Scottish HEIs and has attracted participants from beyond Scotland. Participants have included serving or potential heads of academic and of administrative and support areas. Each part of the programme takes three days. Much of the value of the residential programme stems from the mix of participants, the sharing of experiences, the continuity of contact and the choice of topics and presenters.

Part One focuses upon: discussions of managerial and leadership roles; on managing people and other resources. In connection with the latter, participants hear the viewpoint of the Funding Council from the Director of Funding. The programme starts with a scene-setting from a senior manager, typically a vice-chancellor, or the Chief Executive of the Funding Council.

A senior figure is the opening speaker to Part Two. Thereafter the programme addresses: performance indicators, departmental reviews and departmental effectiveness; the management of change and current aspects of the quality processes. The former is based upon the practice in one institution (Goldsmiths College), whereas the latter is driven by cases provided by participants that are discussed in groups as a means of identifying the nature and processes of the effective management of change. An element of choice in the structure enables participants to select two topical workshops on day two. In the most recent course the workshop topics were strategic planning and resource allocation, employing and managing contract researchers, and equal opportunities.

All sessions are participative, many are arranged in discussion groups. Participants receive pre-course reading materials and select bibliographies. The emphasis on the programme is upon strategic thinking, planning and analysis, awareness-raising, exploring perceptions, problem-sharing and disseminating good practice. It does not seek to offer training in specific skills or feedback on the performance of the participants, although the evaluation forms indicate that many individuals reflect upon their style and effectiveness and plan to make changes.

Additionally, under the aegis of the COSHEP Staff Development Committee, three-day annual induction and middle management courses are held for administrative staff, there is an annual leadership conference (in 1997 the topic is institutional positioning, particularly in relation to teaching and research), and a wide variety of topical courses and workshops, such as financial management, managing and developing contract research staff, managing and developing part-time tutors.

Management development for individuals: London University's Academic Management Programme

The University of London's Academic Management Programme (AMP) is probably one of the oldest surviving programmes for new or relatively inexperienced academic managers (deans and heads of department) in the UK. It originated in the 1970s, with a lapse in the early 1980s, followed by a revival which has lasted for more than ten years (the latest programme was mounted in April 1997). The format of the AMP is traditional, involving academic managers leaving their work for a period of 'structured reflection and awareness-raising' which combines case-studies, exercises, games, lectures, discussion, videos and role-play, co-ordinated and presented by a variety of 'itinerant experts'.

Much of the value of the week-long residential programme is achieved through the combination of distance from the day-to-day task (providing an opportunity to reflect on experience) and the chance to learn from the experience of others in a non-competitive context. In some years, the value has been sustained by continued support being provided by participants to each other in the form of an informal help-line and in supplementary activities where the original group has reformed. Where the programme falls short is in relation to skills training, in the provision of feedback on performance in context, in its potential for changing attitudes to the management task (with some exceptions), and in the integration of management learning and institutional development. The AMP provides one kind of approach to management development, but it needs to be supplemented by other approaches if management and organizational learning are to be achieved.

Group-based development: the Managing for Quality initiative

In 1995, the Higher Education Quality Council published a report of an initiative, aimed at academic heads of departments, entitled *Managing for Quality* which was designed as a case study resource for academic managers and leaders. The initiative was unusual in seeking to bring together a group of experienced academic managers (one participant from each university was invited), not to participate in a course, but to participate in a management learning project. The project was designed by a team of individuals who were involved in management development activities in their institutions and included a number of activities which were developed iteratively in negotiations and feedback between the project team and the academic managers.

The main activities revolved around 'a case' which was written up by each academic manager on the basis of a quality management problem which they had encountered. The case was in the form of: context; description of a problem; problem-solving strategies used and their effect; resources and support needed or sought. These cases were then discussed between small groups of the managers, first in groups of three to gain practical advice and comment on the case, and second, in groups of six to explore whether generic issues could be identified which would throw light on the academic management task more generally. Following these discussions, the cases were revised and sent in to the project team.

The value added by the team was to undertake an analysis of the cases in order to categorize and group them into a variety of management topics and to identify common themes which could be developed further (for example, into a four-step guide to managing change at departmental level and into a checklist on 'good management' practice, drawing on examples from the cases as well as relevant literature). Additional material was provided by the team including a context-setting piece on academic management in the 1990s, an annotated bibliography, and guidance for academic managers on a problem-solving approach which could make use of the project materials on an individual basis or in groups. All these materials were integrated into the full publication which was then made available to all institutions and to staff development networks.

The value of this approach came at several points in the project: in the reflection, analysis and feedback on individual cases, in the discussions about generic themes in quality management, in the development of the various practical 'tools' for assisting managers with their day-to-day tasks, and with managing change and problem-solving more generally, and finally, in the opportunity for further reflection and learning from reading and analysis of the collected cases. However, still greater value could have been achieved if the momentum of the original project (which led to the publication of the cases) had been extended. This might have been done, for example, through the mounting of seminars to draw the attention of other academic managers, and those involved in management development, to the initiative as a model which used 'real-life' scenarios as a basis for learning, or, perhaps, if the original participants of the project had extended their original contacts to build a sustainable learning network.

Institution-based management development: Strathclyde University

A short annual programme for new heads of academic departments commenced in the 1970s. From the outset there was a commitment from senior officers in terms of attendance and contribution. By the mid-1980s the programme had expanded to include workshop sessions that enabled participants to consider their preferred management styles and to perform tasks such as 'in-tray' exercises. The next phase in the evolution was the incorporation of a rolling case study which took a new head of department through a series of events spanning the first two years of office.

Three years ago the two-day residential course was redesigned. Attendance is now expected as part of the contractual terms of appointment to headship. Participants receive an extensive in-house management handbook that itemises policies and procedures. Experienced heads are involved in the design of the programme and act as session leaders and facilitators. Care is taken to ensure that the vice-chancellor can contribute to the programme, a feature much valued by participants.

Substantial sessions deal with: responsibilities, obligations, rights, pressures and skills; leading and managing departments (especially in relation to research and scholarship and teaching and learning); dealing with staff issues; supporting, developing and motivating staff; the planning processes; and financial management and budgetary control. A wide array of additional events are held for managers to cover a number of issues, eg, health and safety.

At the sectional or departmental level retreats have been commonplace, with the emphasis upon development and upon the focusing of departmental strategies and priorities. Within the administration, the scale of the activity involves the event being held at least three times each year.

One significant pilot activity in 1996–97 involved a sustained team-building programme, primarily for one volunteer per large academic department, although places were made available to staff in cognate departments. The team-building activities were integrated into a developmental process for the department which was concerned with achieving greater involvement and more effective operational management. Resource constraints are likely to restrict the extension of this approach to every department, but useful lessons have been learned about the acceptability and potential of the initiative.

As part of the activities associated with the revision of the institutional plan and with work towards recognition by Investors in People, the staff development policy has been revised, appraisal has been extended to further categories of staff, more integrated strategies for staff development are being formulated and accredited programmes, including substantial work-based components, have been validated. The staff development policy identifies the responsibilities of individuals, managers and dedicated support centres. Particular attention has been paid to the central role of heads of department or centres or units. To be accepted as relevant and workable, all of these changes must be consonant both with the institutional aims and objectives and with the devolved system of management that prevails in the University.

Sector-wide development: some perspectives from the Graduate Standards Programme (GSP)

The Graduate Standards Programme represents a series of inter-related investigations and consultations on the topic of academic standards, focusing particularly on the ways in which such standards are established, delivered, measured, monitored and compared across UK higher education. The focus of the programme has not been directly on the managerial role, but many of the processes which have been the focus of attention are part of the responsibilities of academic managers. Indeed, one of the outcomes of the programme has been to identify areas where more effective leadership and management are needed to ensure that standards are maintained and improved and that the expectations of major constituencies (such as students and employers) are addressed.

In the course of the programme, managers have been targeted as key respondents and have therefore been involved in the investigations, consultations and dissemination activities. For example, heads of department are involved in subject networks which are piloting new approaches to the articulation of academic standards in their disciplines; quality assurance managers have been involved in commenting upon key findings, in advising on recommendations for action, in developing specific guidelines or audit tools; and both groups are involved in a variety of development projects. Some are designing new quality assurance frameworks at departmental level, others are engaged in systematic comparisons of institutional practice through the process of 'benchmarking'.

The Graduate Standards Programme has sought to adopt an enhancement-led approach to policy consultation and decision-making by seeking to involve those who will ultimately be responsible for policy development and implementation at local levels. Such an approach allows a focus on the reality of the academic management task, using day-to-day imperatives as a basis not only for management action, but also for management learning and change. The opportunities that have been generated have encouraged analysis and reflection on current practice, have promoted the exchange and discussion of new perspectives and alternative ways of doing things (eg, across disciplines and professional groups), and have stimulated creativity and experiment 'at the coal face'. In this way, sectoral, institutional, cross-disciplinary, and individual learning and change have been addressed and, to some extent, integrated. The approach has the potential to address a major difficulty in organizational development, namely, that many aspects of management require co-ordinated or synchronous development and action across functions where different managers hold sway; the GSP has highlighted the need for a systemic view of management learning and organizational change, not only, of course, across internal functions, but also through making connections with key constituencies and stakeholders.

What next?

In a nutshell, there are several obvious needs in relation to management learning in UK HE: a wider range of provision, impacting upon a much larger number of 'managers'; the use of various modes and forms of learning experience (including self-paced multimedia resources); provisions which address specific 'just-in-time' requirements, be those awareness-raising or skills training, sequenced learning programmes, benchmarking experiences that draw upon examples from within and beyond HE, or planned opportunities for reflection and creative thinking.

The array of modes of learning is increasing rapidly. Computer-based and multimedia packages on facets of management competencies are available and in use, albeit not designed specifically for HE. In a number of institutions, especially medium to large HEIs, more integrated and tailored staff development strategies and accredited offerings are being put in place. Regional and system-wide developments are flourishing, where the benefits of collaboration are deemed to outweigh any limitations and disadvantages that can accrue from multi-institutional training, development and learning endeavours.

The CVCP is considering the introduction of an HE version of the Cabinet Office month-long residential top management course, where the emphasis is upon reflection, with an interweaving of sustained in-depth real case studies and focused presentations.

Many specialist networks such as finance officers, personnel officers, and residence and catering directors, hold annual events which include strong management development and learning components. In addition to the above, endeavours might benefit both from clearer identification of perceived needs and from greater attention to learning styles in the design of learning experiences (Kolb, 1984; Honey and Mumford, 1992). This needs to be aligned to studies of how professionals develop knowledge and competence (see Eraut, 1994).

> Professionals continually learn on the job, because their work entails engagement in a succession of cases, problems or projects which they have to learn about. This case-specific learning, however, may not contribute a great deal to their general professional knowledge base unless the case is regarded as special rather than routine and time is set aside to deliberate upon its significance. Even then it may remain in memory as a special case without being integrated into any general theory of practice.
>
> (Eraut, 1994)

The message from Eraut is clear. Effective learning requires embedding, in effect it involves the personal management of change, be that minor and substantial. That point is certainly not widely acknowledged at present, as evidenced by the commonplace items in a workshop or short course questionnaire which asks participants what they have learned. Many participants validly respond that they are uncertain and will need to reflect upon various things that attracted their interest. The phase that needs strengthening is the supportive follow up to encourage further dialogue, evaluation and selective adoption.

Eraut (1994) summarizes four theories of professional expertise, namely:

- the H. and S. Dreyfus (1986) model of skill acquisition (novice Æ expert);
- theories of clinical decision-making;

- Hammond's (1980) Cognitive Continuum theory; and
- Schön's (1983) *The Reflective Practitioner*.

Eraut draws particular attention to the influence of time and speed in professional work, (echoing Stewart's findings about managerial work described above), stating that deliberation may be more the exception than the rule. Reflecting upon and learning from loosely structured, partly unplanned experiences is a demanding task which can easily be contaminated by *post-hoc* rationalization and tidying.

Eraut favours the use of professional obligations to compulsory schemes. His carefully argued position has to be set alongside that of the views of Madden and Mitchell (1993) arising from their case studies of CPD in a number of professions: 'The disadvantage of all voluntary CPD schemes is that those with the most to gain from continuing their professional learning are usually the least likely to do so.'

Writing on head teachers learning about management, Eraut (1994) identified six facets of knowledge development:

- developing knowledge of people;
- developing situational knowledge;
- developing knowledge of educational practice;
- developing conceptual knowledge;
- developing process knowledge;
- developing control knowledge (with self-management at its core).

Each is informed by detailed insights into learning opportunities and intentions. Wider usage of similar frameworks might enable management development and learning in HE to progress, both in terms of rungs on the ladder proposed by Burgoyne and in enabling participants to access structures against which they can reflect upon their learning needs and experiences. Potentially exciting challenges are opening up as learning for managers and professionals – or for professionals as managers – is integrated with the imperative of 'the learning organization', capable of responding swiftly and appropriately to pressures for change.

References

Andrews Munro (1996) *Executive Audit Profile*, AM Ltd, Chipping Norton.

Baldridge, JV *et al.* (1978) *Policy Making and Effective Leadership*, Jossey-Bass, San Francisco.

Bergquist, WH (1992) *The Four Cultures of the Academy*, Jossey-Bass, San Francisco.

Blake, RR and Mouton, J S (1964) *The Managerial Grid*, Scientific Methods Inc, Texas.

Brown, G and Atkins, M (1986) 'Academic staff training in British universities', *Studies in Higher Education*, vol. 11, no. 1, p. 11.

Burgoyne, J (1988) 'Managerial development for the individual and organisation', *Personnel Management*, June, pp. 40–4.

Cannon, T (1996) *Welcome to the Revolution: Managing Paradox in the Twenty-First Century*, Pitman, London.

Checkland, PB (1981) *Systems Thinking, Systems Practice*, John Wiley, Chichester.

Cohen, MD and March, JG (1974) *Leadership and Ambiguity: The American College President*, McGraw-Hill, New York.

Crosby, P B (1984) *Quality Without Tears: The Art of Hassle-Free Management*, McGraw-Hill, New York.

CVCP (1995) *Learning for Change: Building a University System for the New Century*, CVCP, London.

CVCP *et al.* (1996) *Concordat on Contract Research Staff Career Management*, CVCP, London.

Deal, TE and Kennedy, AA (1982) *Corporate Cultures: The Rites and Rituals of Corporate Life*, Addison-Wesley, Reading, MA.

Deming, WE (1982) *Out of the Crisis*, Productivity Press, Cambridge, MA.

Dreyfus, HL and Dreyfus, SE (1986) *Mind over Machine: The Power of Human Intuition and Expertise in the Era of the Computer*, Blackwell, Oxford.

Duke, C (1992) *The Learning University*, SRHE/OUP, Buckingham.

Eraut, M (1994) *Developing Professional Knowledge and Competence*, Falmer Press, London.

Fayol, H (1949) *General Industrial Management*, Pitman, London (first published 1916).

Gordon, G (1995) 'Higher Education 2005: pointers, possibilities, pitfalls, principles', *Quality Assurance in Education*, vol. 3, no. 4, pp. 21–9.

Gmelch, WH *et al.* (1996) 'A cross-cultural comparison of department chair stress in Australia and the United States', paper presented at ASHE Conference, Memphis.

Hammond, KR *et al.* (1980) *Human Judgement and Decision Making*, Hemisphere, New York.

Hardy, C (1979) *Gods of Management*, Pan, London.

Harrison, R (1972) 'Understanding your organisation's character', *Harvard Business Review*, (May–June), vol. 50, no. 3, pp. 119–28.

Harvey, L (1996), Editorial, *Quality in Higher Education*, vol. 2, no. 3, pp. 107–84.

Henkel, M (1997) 'Academic values and the university as corporate enterprise', *Higher Education Quarterly*, vol. 51, no. 2, pp. 134–43.

Hersey, P and Blanchard, HK (1977) *Management of Organisational Behaviour: Utilising Human Resources* 3rd edn, Prentice-Hall, Englewood Cliffs, NJ.

Honey, P and Mumford, A (1992) *The Manual of Learning Styles*, Honey and Mumford, Maidenhead.

Jarratt, A (1985), *Report of the Steering Committee on Efficiency Studies in Universities*, CVCP, London.

Johnston, RJ (1996) 'Managing how academics manage', in R. Cuthbert (ed.), *Working in Higher Education*, SRHE/OUP, Buckingham.

Juran, JM (1988) *Juran on Planning for Quality*, Free Press, New York.

Kolb, DA (1984) *Experiential Learning: Experience as a Source of Learning*, Prentice-Hall, Englewood Cliffs, NJ.

Kotter, J (1990) *A Force for Change: How Leadership Differs from Management*, Free Press, New York.

Levine, A (1993) 'Students' expectations of college', *Change*, Sept/Oct, p. 4.

Madden, CA and Mitchell, VA (1993) *Professions, Standards and Competencies*, University of Bristol, Bristol.

McCall, MW *et al.* (1988) *The Lessons of Experience*, Lexington Books, Lexington.

McGregor, D (1960) *The Human Side of Enterprise*, McGraw-Hill, New York.

McNay, I (1993) 'The evolving university: four cultural models', paper presented at EAIR Conference, Turku.

Middlehurst, R (1993) *Leading Academics*, SRHE/OUP, Buckingham.

Middlehurst, R *et al* (1995) *Managing for Quality: Stories and Strategies*, HEQC, London.

Mintzberg, H (1973) *The Nature of Managerial Work*, Harper and Row, New York.

Moses, I and Roe, E (1990) *Heads and Chairs: Managing Academic Departments*, University of Queensland, Brisbane.

Partington, P *et al.* (1994) *Higher Education Management and Leadership: Towards a National Framework for Preparation and Development*, UCoSDA, Sheffield.

Pedler, M *et al.* (1991) *The Learning Company*, McGraw-Hill, London.

Peters, T and Waterman, R (1982) *In Search of Excellence*, Harper & Row, New York.

Pollitt, C (1990) *Managerialism and the Public Services: The Anglo-American Experience*, Blackwell, Oxford.

Pollitt, C (1995) 'Justification by works or by faith? Evaluating the new public management', *Evaluation*, vol. 1, no. 2, pp. 133–54.

Sarros, JC, Gmelch, WH and Tanewski, GA (1997) 'The role of department head in Australian universities: changes and challenges', *HERD*, vol. 16, no. 1, pp. 9–24.

Schön, DA (1983) *The Reflective Practitioner*, Maurice Temple-Smith, London.

Schuller, T (ed.) (1995) The Changing University SRHE/OUP, Buckingham.

Senge, P M (1990) *The Fifth Discipline: The Art and Practice of the Learning Organisation*, Century, London.

Stewart, R (1997) *The Reality of Management*, 3rd edition, Butterworth-Heinemann, Oxford.

Stodgill, RM and Coons, AE (eds) (1957) *Leader Behaviour: Its Description and Measurement*, Bureau of Business Research, Ohio University, Columbus, OH.

Taylor, FW (1911) *Principles of Scientific Management*, Harper, New York.

Thorpe, M and Cuthbert, R (1996) 'Autonomy, bureaucracy and competition', in R. Cuthbert (ed.), *Working in Higher Education*, SRHE/OUP, Buckingham.

Watson, REL (1986) 'The role of the department chair: a replication and extension', *The Canadian Journal of Higher Education*, vol. 16, no. 1, pp. 13–23.

Wisker, G. (ed.) (1996) *Leading Academic Programmes and Courses*, SEDA Paper 97, SEDA, Birmingham.

—— 11 ——

Operating staff development effectively in higher education: a departmental perspective

Jenny Wilkinson

Where does the main thrust of staff development activity come from within an institution? Is it generated mainly from central staff development units? What part does a department play in ensuring development and training activity? In answering these questions it would be easy to imagine that central units, and the training and development programmes they offer, constitute the main staff development activities within a university. Closer analysis, however, would probably show that a substantial amount of training and development occurs within individual departments and falls outside the bounds of any central staff development unit. This spread of activity and responsibility is further encouraged in those institutions where the staff development budget is devolved to budget centres, ensuring that a degree of responsibility for training and development exists at a local level.

This chapter is written as a personal observation of someone who moved from being a training and development officer in a central staff development unit to being the departmental administrator of a large department in the same university. It examines the changes in attitude and perspective that I adopted as a result of this transition and discusses how departments can successfully contribute to a programme of staff development.

In particular I shall look at the pros and cons of trying to run a programme of staff development at departmental level and examine whether the devolvement of these activities encourages a more planned approach to staff development, more in touch with the individuals at the local level, or whether it reduces the impact of staff development because it lacks the drive and commitment from the centre.

Department vs central administration

I joined the central staff development unit in my institution when it was established in 1991. We were responsible for building a central training programme for all staff. I had particular responsibility for clerical, technical and manual staff and for the development of IT training programmes. In the early days it was easy to imagine that we were pioneers and that no one had attempted to train the staff before our arrival. Indeed, in some areas, particularly IT, we were heralded almost as 'messiahs of the new dawn'. Events that we presented were well received, especially by the clerical and technical staff, who were always eager for more. When it came to auditing and measuring staff development activity within the university we naturally concentrated on our own activities and counted the number of people who had been on our courses. Despite our best efforts it was clear that many staff in the university were not taking advantage of the training and developmental opportunities on offer. As we investigated this further and liaised with staff we discovered that people were being trained and developed locally within their department, and that much of this activity was unreported. Some staff were being funded by their department to attend training courses whilst others were being mentored by colleagues. Either way, it was important training and developmental activity that could not be ignored.

After four years working within the central administration of the university I moved to take up a position as academic secretary with the School of Education. As part of my newly acquired supervisory role for support and allied staff, I was also responsible for the training and development of these people. From this new vantage point I was able to experience at first hand the difficulties and successes of providing an efficient programme of training and development at departmental level.

Departmental responsibility: the reality

What, in reality, is a department or faculty expected to do or provide in relation to the development of its personnel? This will alter from institution to institution as different universities develop different frameworks for the provision of staff development. In my institution I can identify two key areas where the central administration requires departmental input: the identification of training needs and the reporting of training activities.

Identifying training needs

In my institution, departments, as well as individuals, are expected to identify training needs for staff. Appraisal is the mechanism through which the head of department can do this at a departmental level. The needs are then communicated to the central staff development unit who in turn co-ordinate the combined requirements of the entire institution and investigate ways of delivering the most appropriate response, be it in the form of a training course or another form of developmental activity. This procedure sounds fine in theory, but having worked in both the central staff development unit and in a department, I have been able to watch this process from both perspectives and now have a more realistic understanding of how departments respond to staff in terms of identifying and satisfying training needs.

Appraisal: its role and its uses

It is probably fair to say that even the best intended individuals, who run departments, view the training needs aspect of appraisal as a paper exercise. Indeed, the system encourages this by removing the onus of responsibility from one person and placing it on another half-way through the process. Although the head of department liaises with the individual members of the department to identify training needs, and consequently co-ordinates a departmental response, the process is often then handed over to the central unit who consider all departmental responses and provide a global programme in answer to individual requests. It now becomes their respons-ibility to see the process through to the end and provide the appropriate training. In a system like this the various players can justifiably feel that they have adequately completed all their obligations. The head of depart-ment can feel satisfied that s/he has fulfilled their responsibility to the individual by communicating their requirements to those who can provide the solutions. The staff development unit can feel happy that they have laid on an appropriate programme in accordance with the requests they received. However, there is no guarantee, and probably no follow up, to ensure that the individual member of staff actually attended the relevant course.

Imagine this scenario:

During her appraisal a very shy member of clerical staff admits that she is rather nervous of the phone, especially as one of the academics in the department has been rude to her several times when working at home and has had to be rung to answer some questions. The appraiser is very sympathetic and notes the need for the person to be encouraged to have more confidence in dealing with people. The appraisal is completed and the form is then sent to the head of department for final signature. The head of department notices this problem and asks the appraiser to outline the difficulties. The appraiser indicates that the problem usually arises in relation to using the phone. Consequently the head of department writes a note to the staff development unit asking them for some courses that cover confidence in using the phone.

The staff development unit receive the information on training needs from all departments and notice that there are several people for whom the telephone appears to be a problem – consequently, they organize a course on telephone skills.

Meanwhile, back in the department, the clerical assistant waits for the new staff development programme to be announced so that she can book on to the courses on confidence building and dealing with difficult people. She is, however, disappointed when the programme arrives as there is no mention of such a course and her eyes quickly skim over the telephone course which she went on two years ago as part of her induction programme.

The start of the process and the end result are so far apart that the individual fails to make the connection or see the relevance of the centrally provided programme to their circumstances. A further consequence of this is that attendance on courses may not be as high as was hoped as the staff for whom they were intended do not attend. Liaison between staff, the department and the staff development unit is a vital part of delivering suitable and appropriate training. It should not be left solely to the mechanism of such things as appraisal.

Reporting training activities: training logs

As I mentioned earlier, we quickly discovered that staff development activity within our institution was not limited to the training programmes provided by the central staff development unit. It was understood that all manner of activities including mentoring, attending a conference, reading a book, etc constituted staff development. In order to recognize this and to provide a more accurate picture of staff participation in training and personal development, a system of training logs was introduced. All members of university staff are now expected to keep a log of all training attended by themselves within the year. Heads of departments are charged with the responsibility of viewing these training logs and sending a summary report to the staff development unit at the end of the year. To make things easier in my department I have created a simple database to record the many varied activities that the staff wanted to report. This can then produce simple summaries and spot trends of activities. This process has helped to raise the profile of staff development and enabled a more complete and accurate picture to be recorded. However, many staff have objected, suggesting that such an audit was an unnecessary bureaucratic exercise. This, then, is another example of a process which is perceived centrally as being very instructive and of value, yet is seen locally as little more than a nuisance by staff in the department.

So . . . what is the role of the department?

In answer to the question that started this section, departmental responsibility can, in reality, be little more than the completion of a paper exercise, either as a written request to a central unit outlining the training requests of its staff, or as a reporting exercise detailing activities that have happened. As I see it, there is rarely a specific requirement for the department to pursue a pro-active programme of activities to develop the staff. Equally, departments are not officially required to monitor the development of staff or notice the transfer of skills into the workplace. In other words, there is no onus on the department to assess the success or otherwise of staff training and no requirement to provide opportunities in which the development of staff can flourish. This is a shame, and a missed opportunity because it would seem to me that the best place to monitor progress and assess need is in the department, at the grass roots-level, not in a distant, central unit.

Devolving staff development to departments: the dangers

If we are to continue this line of argument and pursue the idea that departments are best placed to assess training needs and monitor staff development, then we must ask the following question: are budget centres and departments fully equipped and resourced to deal effectively with staff development at a local level? An effective staff development programme needs to be co-ordinated by people who are skilled in identifying training needs, able to monitor progress and can provide an environment under which continuous improvement can be nurtured and encouraged.

The success of this would rely on the identification of a person based locally who could be responsible for staff development, and I would question whether all departments are able to do this. Without some sort of overseeing co-ordination, staff development becomes little more than a bidding process by individuals attempting to gain financial support for courses they wish to attend. This is not strategic or planned. A few individuals may benefit, but others will miss out and the departmental and institutional needs will almost certainly be ignored.

Where co-ordinators can be identified, we then have to consider whether they are skilled in identifying staff training needs. Will they take the time, or indeed be allowed to take the time, to adopt a long-term, strategic view of training needs? Or will they simply become a gatekeeper to the money – monitoring expenditure rather than success?

During a recent interview to appoint a senior member of clerical staff, with supervisory responsibility for a team of four, candidates were asked how they would identify training needs. The answers illustrated very clearly the two extremes of my concern. The first candidate answered, 'Well, I would ask them what courses they wanted to go on and then see if the staff development unit were offering courses they wanted and then let them go.' The second candidate approached the question from a completely different angle, saying, 'Well, I would look at the job and see where improvements could be made and send people on courses accordingly.' Both these candidates were well meaning, and, in their own way, committed to staff development and training. However, the first was steered too much by the individual desire and the second too concerned about the task in hand rather than the person. Thankfully, the third candidate said that they would combine individual requests with careful monitoring of team performance to identify where efficiency could be enhanced.

One of the major problems of using staff within the department is that, unless they have been trained themselves in the development of staff, they may have a very blinkered view of what it means to train and develop a person. Many would see the answer to all problems as sending someone on a training course, and, as any good staff developer knows, a training course is just one possible solution out of many alternative strategies that can be used to develop staff.

Another concern about relying on departments heavily for staff training is that the resources available may be too small. By the time staff development budgets have been devolved down to every department within a large faculty, they may amount to little more than enough to buy a couple of books on time management. There is a strong argument here for keeping the budget centrally so that resources can be pooled to enable the staff developers within the institution to run programmes on more than a shoe-string.

My final concern is that an over-concentration on department responsibility could lead to individuals within the department being barred from staff development activities. It is not unknown for senior staff within departments to prevent other staff from attending courses, usually on the grounds that the course or activity is not relevant to the job. Whilst the reasons for stopping people's participation may be legitimate, the fact remains that the more power the department has in this area, the more this is likely to happen. With a central staff development programme staff can individually request to attend courses. Any refusal by the department to allow its staff to attend would then be noticeable and there is a chance that continuous, unnecessary refusals could be discussed and hopefully prevented.

Devolving staff development to departments: the opportunities

Having considered the negative aspects of allowing departments to take a major hand in organizing their own staff development we should now look at the positive aspects. One of the most obvious benefits is the immediacy of the locally based staff developer to the staff in question and the insight this gives them into both the training needs and the success of any programmes which are set up.

In some ways it could be argued that staff development is only truly successful when it is run at a local level. Central staff development courses are all very well and they offer staff the opportunity to spend some time reflecting on their work practices and efficiency but, on the whole, such courses are run in a vacuum. They have little to do with the office or laboratory environment back in the department and very little of what is covered during the session or activity can be transferred directly back to the workplace. Certainly it is almost impossible to monitor the success of centrally run courses in terms of improved working practice or departmental benefit (unless the course was covering a particular, measurable, skill such as IT). Clearly, one of the benefits of running programmes locally is their immediacy to the staff concerned and the opportunities this provides for monitoring progress in the workplace and measuring the impact that the training has on the everyday work experience of the people involved.

The knowledge gained from working closely with people enables a staff developer operating locally to have an excellent insight into the problems and difficulties experienced by staff. Consequently, it is possible to adapt training materials and tailor training events to make them very appropriate to the people attending. I can recall several occasions when, working for the Staff Development Unit, I endeavoured to create case studies which were relevant to the trainees, only to find that they were wide of the mark for at least 25 per cent of those attending. The range of the people attending, and the experiences they brought with them from their different departments, made this an almost impossible task. Working with a group of people from the same department means that it is much easier to focus on issues that affect them. The training is therefore appropriate to the needs of the individuals and appropriate training must be more effective than a generalized approach.

Part of my role within the department in which I now work is to develop not only the clerical and technical staff, but also the office practices and procedures. Staff developers often see themselves as agents of change, but when you work centrally and at a distance from your trainees, the impact that you have is reduced once the trainee returns to their department. Often they will be the only person from their area to have attended. Putting a new way of working into practice can be an uphill struggle especially if their colleagues don't understand what they are doing. Alternatively, when you work at the coal face alongside your trainees the ideas that you are trying to introduce will have a greater degree of relevance. Furthermore, you can ensure that whole offices and teams are trained together so that all members of the office have a shared experience and can bring the training ideas back to the department and develop a joint response to them. Even subjects that are very personal, such as assertiveness and time management, are easier to put into practice when the whole office has an understanding of what they entail. When I trained people centrally I frequently received the comment on the assessment forms that the course was great and they learnt a lot, but how do they get the rest of the department to understand the issues and the benefits of that particular session?

Finally, I would suggest that working within a department as a staff developer provides you with a unique opportunity to create a culture and an environment in which learning and practising taught techniques are acceptable. So often staff would tell me that they didn't have time to practise the skills they had learnt, particularly in relation to IT. Consequently, much of the benefit they gained from the training was rapidly lost. It isn't easy to get people to transfer new skills to their everyday lives, but it is more likely to be effective if you can create an environment where they believe it is safe and appropriate to try.

Operating staff development in the department efficiently: the difficulties

Attempting to operate a staff development programme at a local level makes me acutely aware of what staff think about training and development and how difficult it is to offer an efficient programme.

The first difficulty I have is with myself and finding the time to develop suitable training responses for the needs of the staff in the department. My new role is not solely dedicated to staff development and it is very unlikely that any post at department or faculty level would be. We will always have other things to do which are apparently more important and it is very easy to be drawn in to the trap of thinking, 'it's only a bit of staff training – it doesn't really matter', especially when the pressure is on to perform in some other aspect of your role. I believe it is vital to spend time building the skills of the clerical and technical staff in my area, therefore it is important that I give staff development a high priority, but this is not always easy to achieve.

The practical problems of allowing people the time to develop themselves are more obvious when you work within a department and you become acutely aware of the 'hidden' cost of training. You realize the need to provide cover for key areas of the department, such as reception, when the receptionist requires time to support her or his training and development. Organizing a development day for all the clerical staff to attend becomes a major operation and requires planning to military precision to ensure that the department does not grind to a halt. You become more aware of the disruption time out of the office can cause. This in turn makes me highly aware of the responsibility I have to offer training events which are relevant and effective. The cost involved is not limited to that which is spent on providing coffees, lunches and teas, but the salary of each and every person who spends the day, afternoon or morning with you. It is important therefore to get it right. In some ways the pressure of operating locally is enhanced because you have a much higher level of responsibility to the people involved.

It is, however, not appropriate to run some training events locally. On a recent development day which I ran with the clerical staff within my department I was aware that there were certain people who were finding it difficult to open up and express their thoughts. I realized, of course, that these people would probably welcome the opportunity to discuss certain issues with relative strangers and that maybe we were all a little too close to home. Certain courses will not be affected by this, such as skill-based IT training courses, but I will probably never attempt to run a course on Dealing with Difficult People locally – after all, I may well be their difficult person! It is important to recognize that certain issues are better dealt with away from colleagues and the work environment.

One final problem, which is not an issue for me as we have over 30 allied and support staff within the department, is the limited number of staff that support the work of a department. Many departments exist with just one or two members of part-time staff. Clearly local implementation of a training programme in this situation would have to be done at faculty level, and this may be too far removed from the people concerned to maintain the benefits described earlier. For those individuals who work alone, the opportunity of attending a central course provides a unique chance to network with other people who are doing similar jobs. Even in a large department there will only be one senior secretary or one chief technician. Only central courses or something co-ordinated by the centre will enable them to meet other staff working at the same level as themselves.

Departmental training and the role of the central staff development unit

With devolvement of staff development on the increase we must consider what this means for the central staff development units. Clearly, they should continue to operate, and should not be sized down as part of any cost saving exercise. There is still a great need for institutions to have a central location for staff development resources. Staff developers who work within the central administration of an institution could take on the very important and necessary role of advisor to staff at departmental level, offering help and resources to people like myself who are trying to train their staff. Personally, I would not like to see any decrease in the number of centrally run courses as I think they supplement what can be offered by the department and indeed offer an extra dimension in terms of training away from the office, laboratory, workshop, etc. As I mentioned earlier, there are some topics that are better tackled away from the workplace and possibly with a group of people that you don't know and are unlikely to see again. Staff development units should maintain libraries of materials that can be used by staff within the institution for their development.

I do not see the devolvement of staff development as commensurate with the demise of central units. Indeed, I consider staff development units have much to offer in terms of support, advice and consultancy to those of us who are struggling away at the grass roots of the institution. It is good to know that we can call on a central reserve of expertise for advice and assistance.

Conclusions

A recent survey by Fenman Training, reported in the magazine *Management Skills and Development* in April 1997, suggests that trainers are facing a challenging and uncomfortable future as on-the-job training increases at the expense of traditional 'stand-up and deliver training'. Trainers were being seen as facilitators and training budgets were being decentralized.

I would suggest that many universities would not find this a worrying prospect as it represents a situation that has long applied to academic institutions, almost since the rise of staff development activity in the late 1980s. It would seem that, for once, universities are perhaps ahead of the game, and have already contended with the prospect of high departmental involvement in training and development activities.

It is important for institutions to recognize and encourage the benefits that can be gained from efficient and appropriate training operating at departmental level. Central units in turn should consider what they can do to support this and regard it as an extension of their activity rather than a threat to it.

——12——

A staff developer's perspective

Ian Hewes

Arriving in a university to develop its staff can be daunting. Any new initiative faces difficulties, but here the environment is a strange one: the structures, habits and language of universities are all their own. The features that have enabled universities to survive longer than most other large organizations can militate against change. Some groups within a university see an interest in staff development and want to turn it their own way. Others resist it. What do the various groups of staff want? How does one understand what is going on enough to decide what to do? And how will it all work out? This chapter contemplates the view from the staff developer's office.

The staff developer can draw support from people and direction from vision and ideas. Colleagues in other universities and national organizations are engaged in the same enterprise; they are a reassurance and a resource. Various theories of organizational psychology and organization development make sense of the environment and guide action when consensus is absent. Most important to the staff developer are colleagues within the university who share an understanding: that the organization can best further many of its goals through the personal engagement and development of its members of staff.

In general, the pioneering phase of staff development in universities is over. The rational phases are in progress. Will the enterprise get stuck here or proceed towards the developmental phase? That will be resolved in individual universities as they choose whether to organise staff development so that it can be responsive to individuals and groups or to control it strictly from the centre for short-term impact on efficiency.

Starting off

Where do you start when you arrive in a university as its first staff development specialist? The senior people who established the post all had their own views as to what was needed. They approved of your ideas at the selection interview, and since then visits and discussions have turned into outline plans in your mind. You know what you think should happen. Then the distractions of reality start. Several colleagues have been looking forward to handing over to you tasks that are clearly within your brief. You wouldn't have done any of them that way yourself, but their temporized methods have become convention. You decide to continue them initially until you see more of the picture.

You talk to the sponsors of your new post and find out again what they want out of it. They seem to have very clear ideas but, again, it seems to you, you wouldn't do it like that. You ask heads of various administrative and academic departments and some of their people what they need. There may be mismatch between the sponsors' agenda and the needs perceived by the prospective clients. If there is a mismatch you add it to the growing list of big things to tackle, but rather than do that now you set up some courses to meet a few of the commonest needs. When courses work well, demand builds quickly for more of the same and for the same treatment for new topics. You have to be careful not to over-stimulate demand – if it exceeds too much the capacity to satisfy it, the result is considerable frustration with staff development. In this respect you can't win.

You begin setting up systems too. The hard systems are for records and budgets, the soft ones are networks of contacts, advisory or regulatory committees. In between are rules for prioritizing requests, methods of evaluation, needs analysis and so on. Each of these processes depends on others at various stages, so it's all fits and starts. There isn't much to show in the way of organizational change.

They have given you some money to spend, but what procedures! However smooth they may be, they're new to you and you have to learn to work them. In any case, spending wisely takes time, the most strained resource. Other resources? There's no training room and it's difficult to book anything decent during term for two hours, let alone for a day at a time. The teaching timetable works in single hours and that's the basis for all room booking other than yours. If you book the conference centre your budget will be gone in a couple of months. So eking out the budget begins straight away.

By now your initially rosy view of the university may be taking on more realistic colours. Like all others, your university is an imperfect manifestation of its type. Sometimes you think nobody would miss it, but they would. It is worth something; its lofty ideals are important. To staff developers a university offers a very unusual place in which to work: like a school, it ought in some ways to be a sort of model society. Certainly it ought to embody the values it expounds. It ought to respect learning as personal growth whether in the lecture room, the library, the workshop, the office or part of the staff development programme. In practice you find that support for this principle is far from universal. Another aspect of the model society one might expect universities to show is trust and respect for the individual. Again, the principle is widely preached but practice is patchy. Consequently, customer care is not always what it might be. And while academics might debate the extent to which students are customers, they are likely to find them behaving more like commercial customers as they bear ever more of the total cost of their education.

New impressions are pretty tiring. The demands of various stakeholders can draw you into short-term thinking or cause you to lose your bearings. Things may be more difficult because the university has not had a staff development officer before and that role is new to you also. Expectations are not clear, perhaps on either side. Others have conventions of behaviour to follow. Even the Vice-Chancellor had a predecessor and has seen other vice-chancellors at work for years. And many others have readily measurable work: lists of publications, numbers of clients served, projects dealt with, hours taught. These measures do not exist for your work, especially in the early stages. Even the later measures suggested – numbers of courses arranged, people attending, and so on – do not indicate the spread of the message or the effectiveness of the courses but the volume of the busy work.

You were hired because you understand something about staff development. You know that staff development isn't a set of procedures or a programme of courses, but an attitude, a set of values. Others may not see this. They may not be aware that the task they have implicitly set staff development is to spread those values and attitudes, in fact to change the whole organization. Generally, they do not want to hear this either. Many take the understandable line, 'You're the expert – get on with it.'

The answer, of course, is to do just that. You respond to requests, but try to keep the ideal goals in mind. Give people what they want, but aim always to build up soft systems to improve the development of needs, so that they reflect not the immediate whim of a boss, but the considered needs of a group, linked to institutional goals and values. This means encouraging groups to reflect on their own needs and where possible to meet them from their own resources.

Views of staff development: categories of staff

Staff developers and others who have worked elsewhere agree that universities can be bizarre places. The atmosphere can resemble that of a voluntary organization and some of the cultural patterns are similar. The decision-making process can be labyrinthine. There is a wide diversity of work cultures, in some respects a sort of caste structure, especially in that it is very rare for someone to move from one staff category to another. The cultural differences between staff groups are readily apparent: different styles of language, different habits of communication, different dress, different conditions of service, different working hours, different levels of autonomy. The degree of identification with the institution can vary with staff category. If people when away from work are asked what they do, do they give their specialism or their place of work? If someone says 'I'm a biologist' or 'I'm a fitter' or 'I'm a surveyor', they might be considered to regard themselves more as a member of a discipline, craft or profession than as a member of a specific organization. On the other hand, if they say 'I work at the university' their self-image might be more tightly linked to the idea of the specific organization. Another way of looking at this might be the average distance from their birthplace to the university of members of the different groups. One might expect surveys to confirm the assumption that the higher the status or the narrower the specialism of the group, the greater the average birthplace distance. Whatever their relative status, however, deep commitment to the university and its ideals can be observed in members of all staff groups.

It is possible that the rigidities of caste systems are least visible to members of the highest caste. If this is so, it is not surprising that only a few of the differences in universities' work cultures have attracted the attention of the anthropologists and sociologists of higher education: they are, after all, academics themselves. Becher, Kogan, Hanson and others describe similarities and differences between academic tribes, but their analyses, although fascinating, are largely horizontal and confined to the top of the caste structure. Nevertheless, attention could usefully also be paid to groups who influence other aspects of the experience of students and others working in universities – the non-academic staff. Indeed, the elimination of all unnecessary differences in employment conditions and symbolic status seems likely to add to organizational health by increasing the proportion of staff whose value and dignity are respected. How to achieve such things is pretty well understood, so presumably it is the will that is missing. The superiority of the brahmins is not to be questioned.

The concept of caste may be useful in examining the different ways in which categories of staff respond to staff development. One major difference is in the initial demand for staff development from various staff groups. Hierarchical position may explain such differences. Often staff development is a stigma for academics: participation is somehow an admission of failure. On this view the other side of academic freedom is self-reliance and professional perfection. Below the academic caste there is a divide which may be related to the predominant gender in various groups. Generalist administrators accept management development and personal development. Specialists at professional and craft level often stand on their initial qualification and assert that it is enough for a lifetime. Secretarial and clerical staff seem generally to be keen to take any opportunity there is. Technicians include both the macho rejecters and those open to the most challenging ideas and activities. Manual staff are frequently left out of the equation entirely; they say, 'I didn't think things like that were supposed to be for us.' Sometimes their bosses have given them that impression. Once the opportunity is open, however, keenness, immense talent and enormous untapped potential become evident in many people in all staff groups. Napoleon must have seen something similar to observe that every soldier of France had a field marshal's baton in his knapsack.

In some groups quite a lot of listening and talking is necessary to find activities and circumstances that appeal to all concerned, but happily levels of demand all rise when people are offered courses and other activities that help them with the problems they face. In general, it is fairly easy to whip up demand like this, but unless it can be satisfied it only brings latent frustration. One danger in the start-up period of a staff development unit is that demand and capacity are not developed in parallel.

Generalizations about staff groups obviously conceal a wide range of individual responses. Many staff are keen to do their present job better or want to improve their chances of a better job, often within the university. Many are surprised by staff development and get a taste for things that improve their performance and increase the interest they take in the aims and work of different parts of the organization. Many are delighted that the institution actually permits and promotes activities that are interesting and enjoyable as well as useful.

Views of staff development: managers' attitudes

It is worth looking at some of the attitudes to staff development adopted by managers. Those who have had a hand in establishing the staff development function naturally want it to be seen to be effective. This may mean that they want a long list of courses to prove it's worthwhile. The trouble with this is that a list of opt-in courses may not accord with demand. Some courses will be oversubscribed, many will have to be cancelled. It is not unknown in universities where staff development is programme-based for over half a programme of courses to be cancelled, wasting a lot of initial effort and also doing so publicly. Sometimes explaining the danger of untargeted provision can get these managers involved in analysing the needs of their teams. Often, however, they need more attention before they elaborate their staff development practice and stop wanting to leave everything to the specialist.

Other managers do not understand or respect the process of change. Purposeful management probably can be impatient, but it is unrealistic to believe that changes in a system can be achieved as soon as the need for them is identified. Nevertheless, one-touch managers think that identifying the required behaviour change is enough to achieve it. Others do not see the need for systematic change at all; they think improvement can be brought about by changing the behaviour of single individuals, who then become scapegoats for the eventual failures.

Such short-sighted managers often perceive a need that is not the deepest problem. The action they request may remove the symptom but may not work at all. For example, someone running a service operation may ask for a particular supervisor to be trained in customer care. While this might reduce complaints initially, it might be more helpful for the aims and management of the service to be revised to support the required change. Unless this is done, the poor supervisor goes for training but back on the job does not receive any more support than before. Bosses and others have the same ideas and habits: they still want do things as before. The supervisor has come to realize what the customers want but cannot deliver it and is frustrated. The customers do not perceive any improvement. Managers are tempted to blame the supervisor's motivation or the training.

Staff developers are used to recognizing that a manager's request for a course for someone is often an individually focused expression of a collective need. Some managers do not like hearing this; others are glad to persist, and refine the problem definition so as to be able to take appropriate action.

Many managers understandably want to concentrate on things that will clearly improve the bottom line. Some, seeing a particular change as the principal objective of the moment, are impatient of the means required to bring about lasting improvement, particularly the changes in individuals' behaviour required to achieve it. A group of people needs to be trained in a particular skill, so they are instructed to turn up for training. Surprisingly, some of them often learn something useful and apply it subsequently in their work.

Happily, many managers are well disposed to those they manage, respect individuals' rights to seek some fulfilment at work and are prepared to work together with staff developers to encourage personal growth and improvement in performance.

All groups of staff and all managers have something to gain from staff development. As other parts of the present book show in detail, staff development can reduce people's isolation, improve their awareness of others in the organization, give them a perspective on their work, help them value it more, increase their motivation, draw attention to what they do and attract recognition for it, improve their job prospects and bring them more responsibility. In short, it can stimulate both personal growth and professional effectiveness.

External relations

The staff developer's particular view of the somewhat baffling complexity of the university and various difficulties and its frustrations is generally not shared within the organization, so colleagues in other universities are particularly important. Contact with them is essential. They confirm one's view and help to make sense of it. The atmosphere at conferences of staff developers seems to have an element of relief as people rediscover that the aspects of their language and thoughts that are not generally shared at work are the currency of the specialist gathering. More prosaically the conferences provide all sorts of ideas and practical advice.

The Universities' and Colleges' Staff Development Agency (UCoSDA) is one of the focal organizations for staff developers. One of UCoSDA's most valuable activities has been the promotion of national and regional networks of staff developers. Regional co-operation is efficient as well as congenial.

Other valuable networks operate too. Some are formal – the Association of University Administrators, the Staff and Educational Development Association, regional administrative training committees and so on. Various e-mail mailbase lists are a vital part of understanding what's going on in tedious as well as exciting aspects. The links sections of the various staff development units' web sites are increasingly indispensable. Other networks are of course informal and operate face-to-face as well as by phone and other means. As well as staff developers these often include personnel, external relations and trade union people as well as consultants and others.

The way through the maze

What guides the staff developer through the maze is a compass of vision and a map of theory. One of the qualifications a staff developer ought to start with is a vision of what good staff development is, what an organization that has it can look like and the kinds of behaviour that can bring it about. This vision might take the form of recollections of instances of good practice in your previous organizations or of unconscious theory. The visions of the ideal state and the ways individuals can bring it about may relate to Senge's (1990) delineation of the learning organization in *The Fifth Discipline* and Schön's (1983) description of *The Reflective Practitioner*; but if the visions have grown from experience they may well pre-date the books.

Before joining the university the staff developer has probably worked in large organizations, most likely in the public sector, possibly in other sectors of education. This background is an advantage; it reduces the time needed to become accustomed to the complex values, goals and decision-making patterns of a university. Other background knowledge helps the newcomer. Knowledge of principles and practicalities of finance and management might be considered basic, but the organization is still likely to seem bizarre to a newcomer. One of the things you have to acquire as quickly as possible is a knowledge of the work of various staff groups in the university.

As well as vision the staff developer needs theories through which to understand the events and dynamics of the organization, ideas that suggest relationships between observable phenomena, ideas that can be tested and used to plan and guide action. These are theories of the individual and theories of organizations and groups. Theories of the individual are about personality, growth, learning, motivation, leadership, and so on. Theories of organizations and groups are about intra-group and inter-group dynamics, organizational design and development and organizational culture.

The most useful theory of all is the notion of ownership, central to the thinking of all staff developers and other consultants. If some system that makes sense is not working, it is probably because the people operating it do not own it. Conversely, a system operating well is one to which its operators are committed. How do you encourage people to own a process, a strategy, a goal or a value? By giving them the opportunity to take part in shaping it, to take a share of the responsibility for the outcome. In practice, that means they need information, freedom and sometimes encouragement to contribute their skill or judgement. One of the many consequences is that they understand the work more, are more committed and more capable of initiative and autonomous action. This view of ownership has lots of corollaries: flat management structures need everyone to take more responsibility; trusting people engages them more in their work; managers who sow trust reap commitment, initiative and responsibility.

All the motivation theories confirm the common-sense view that arm-twisting does not foster ownership. So, how do you unfreeze opposition to a given change? The most powerful tool is information. When qualitative and quantitative data are stacked up against the views or behaviour of people resistant to the change in hand, something has to give if they are to maintain consistency among their attitudes, beliefs and behaviour. It is hard to keep thinking of yourself as a reasonable person if your actions are shown widely to be considered unreasonable.

Stages of acceptance of staff development

Another indispensable tool is an idea of the phases in an organization's acceptance of staff development. Various discussions of such phases have appeared in the literature of staff and organization development. What is needed is a model identifying the stages of organizational maturity in particular as regards staff development. A brief outline of a three-phase model can illustrate this. The first and *pioneering stage,* is one in which there is no formal provision for staff development, nor does it figure as a topic in the official discussions of the organization. However, some individuals with management responsibilities bring on their people in various ways, sending them on external courses, coaching, and so on. Others in the organization are aware that in those areas morale is high and people get on well. Gradually the good habits of the pioneers are noted and copied.

The beginning of the second and *rational stage* occurs when some structures are set up to institutionalize the good habits. In universities the establishment of staff development units was also prompted by CVCP and funding bodies. The rational phase is characterized by central developments, that is central to the university rather than in departments. Here the organization acknowledges the importance of staff development and establishes structures and rules to administer it. There are internal courses, systems for identifying developmental needs, channels for communication about staff development and some developmental activities other than courses.

The third phase, which might be called *distributed*, has hard and soft aspects. In the hard aspect of this phase the procedural elements from the foregoing rational phase are present in great quantity, widely distributed through the organization and maintained and controlled by the departments that operate them rather than central authority. The soft aspect of the third phase is the attitudes and behaviour of individuals. People value development for themselves, their colleagues and especially for staff for whose work they are responsible. Nearly all managers have a coaching style and many individuals consciously plan their own development and take action to further it, often by selecting courses and other developmental activities for themselves. Teams, committees and other working groups normally spend time reflecting on their practice and modifying it. They regularly build in evaluation of their projects and processes, discussing how an activity can be done so that it can be learnt from. Rational systems are necessary but not considered the essence of staff development. The behaviour which in the initial phase was pioneering is now normal. Pioneers still exist but they are ahead again, spreading and renewing the messages of reflection, consciousness and growth, stimulating the consideration of ways in which the organization can develop with its members.

Organizations seem to get stuck if the hard and soft elements are not in balance. If the soft is emphasized without the procedural, it fails to take root, wastes effort and gradually loses impact. There are no systems in place to deliver what the organization and its members have grown to want; frustration may result. On the other hand, if the hard is emphasized without consideration of individuals' needs, the procedures become hollow and the institutional goals can lose employee commitment. This can happen if managers insist that staff development is very closely and exclusively related to short-term institutional goals.

Another danger is that the majority thinks that staff development efforts are already sufficient: they recognize that staff development is a good thing, mainly for others, and leave those with designated responsibility to get on with it. In these circumstances management has constantly to seek fresh ways of renewing the effort and mission of the organization. The pursuit of institutional goals needs to be accompanied by managerial commitment to individuals and the development of ownership, participation and trust.

Organizations can get stuck in a particular phase or even regress, but the main danger is not of rolling backwards but of losing momentum and getting bogged down either in sterile procedures or in insubstantial missionary zealotry.

The phase model of change has the weaknesses of many phase models: phases other than the current one are unimaginable; phases overlap in time; they exist side by side in different parts of the organization; transitional stages sometimes seem to be a mixture of many phases. Nevertheless, the model can be a useful way of recognizing the present stage and future direction of development for an organization or part of it.

What next?

What is the current state of progress in universities in terms of this model? Many universities are currently engaged in consolidating the rational stage. In many others, particularly the new universities, the distributed phase is very well advanced. Here the features of the rational phase are firmly in place. Staff development units have been established and well resourced, and are strongly supported by management. Often the units have a formal role in quality assurance, especially if the university is participating in Investors in People. The former polytechnics have been well ahead of other universities in the development of academic staff in educational matters; most have long-established educational methods units. Many of these units have gradually acquired wider responsibilities for staff development.

Now many central units are being reorganized. The main pattern of change is decentralization. Faculties, schools or departments now have either to provide their own services or to purchase them, either from providers outside the university or from the central unit that now has to compete commercially. The direction of this change, towards widespread ownership of provision, is clearly progressive in intention. But unless it is preceded by widespread ownership of the needs for the services, decentralization is likely merely to disperse and dilute effort and expertise. Specialists view hasty devolution with dismay.

The intention that staff development should be widely owned and managed ultimately by its consumers is clearly good. But in learning organizations, where the hard and soft aspects of the distributed phase are in balance, the prevailing management style must be participative. It has to devolve responsibility as well as means. It can do this if the goals of the organization are clear throughout and if commitment to them is widespread.

Unfortunately a participative management style is not widespread in many of the big universities now hurriedly pushing the responsibility and money for staff development out to departments. Here too the medium of management's control is often financial: the allocation of resources and the measurement of performance. Often there is an insistence that the central staff development unit should stand on its own feet like other departments. Academic departments generate their own revenue – fee and research income. Similarly, the staff development unit has to pay for itself by the sale of its services to internal clients.

When the background to this structure is a general shortage of resources and dwindling government support, things can feel pretty desperate to staff developers. They may feel they have to generate money by selling courses outside the university, diverting resources from grants for research projects, by external consultancy. Also they may feel under pressure to spend time and money on the presentation of their own offering as off-the-peg courses in glossy brochures that departments can compare with those of external providers, when previously they had prided themselves on collaborating with departments on high quality tailor-made activities.

Many staff developers are becoming deeply frustrated at having to invest huge energies within the university in presentation, marketing, mass prod-uction, wheeler-dealing and the packaging of aspects of development as research projects to get grant money, while serving external clients for fees. These efforts are not directly related to their true purpose and main aim.

In universities whose staff development units do not charge for their services, the pressure on budgets is increasing as the unit of resource falls. At the same time the pressure for more services is rising and seems unlikely to fall again.

In client departments too there is a more widespread recognition of the role of staff development in supporting change. In particular far more managers see staff development as a tool in the institution's kit. They are keen to relate all staff development to the bottom line. Nothing should be undertaken or supported, they appear to think, unless it relates directly to the immediate priorities of the institution. If people with such views are in high positions or form a high proportion of middle managers, staff devel-opers can feel considerable pressure from yet another direction. Why is this? Surely it is right for staff development efforts to support the institution? Why else should the university spend money on staff development? Surely the purpose of the staff development unit is not to provide amusements, to indulge idlers' self-development, or to reassure weak performers and support misfits and malcontents? Of course not. The aim of the staff development units is to bring about a state of affairs in which individuals develop their own capacity to work. Providing individuals with support and solutions helps them recognize the importance of development; then they can start to take it on.

One of the difficulties in such institutions is that the poorer managers have no sooner realized that staff development exists than they're blaming it for not having sorted out all the organization's problems already. When teaching quality assessors draw attention to potential by saying – as they often do – that staff development could bring about desirable changes, they may unintentionally be adding fuel to the flames. Staff development makes a good scapegoat where it is not recognized as part of every manager's responsibility.

What is the answer to this problem? Not by formal procedures but by widening the ownership of the university's staff development efforts, so that it is in the hands of the people who use it not only for their own personal growth but also for their work. There is no short cut through the natural processes of change but staff development does help to bring about circumstances in which they can go ahead. Staff developers themselves cope with change by a related process, building consensus around what works and choosing like-minded colleagues to work with. Staff developers build networks of people with similar values or vision. This contact is strengthening to everybody involved and gives momentum to the changes. Momentum is everything.

Arranging things so that people take ownership of staff development issues is not always easy or quick. An aside in an e-mail contribution to a staff development mailing list shows both the writer's frustration and her success: 'One of the things that's currently driving me mad is having to listen to people learning, discovering and announcing as Great Exciting New Truths the things that I knew when I arrived here seven years ago and that I've been telling them about and showing them ever since.' The *Tao Te Ching* puts it slightly differently: a description of various types of leader finishes like this: 'Of the best leader, people say after his work is done, "*We* did it ourselves."'

Further reading

Key works

Handy, C (1986) *Understanding Organisations*, Penguin, Harmondsworth.
Schön, DA (1983) *The Reflective Practitioner*, Maurice Temple-Smith, London.
Schein, EH (1988) *Organisational Psychology*, 3rd edn, Prentice-Hall, Englewood Cliffs, NJ.
Senge, PM (1990) *The Fifth Discipline*, Century Business/Random Century, London.

Anthropological views of universities

Becher, T (1989) *Academic Tribes and Territories*, SRHE/Open University Press, Buckingham.
Becher, T and Kogan, M (1980) *Process and Structure in Higher Education*, Heinemann, London.
Hanson, J (1995) 'Hunters and gatherers among the tribes of academe', *New Academic*, vol. 4, no. 1, pp. 12–13.

Phase models

For a general view of phases of organizational maturity see:
Lessem R (1989) *Global Management Principles*, Prentice-Hall, Englewood
    Cliffs, NJ.

For a phase model of (academic) staff development in universities, see:
Brown G *et al.* (1994) *Staff Development for Teaching and Learning: Towards a
    Coherent and Comprehensive Approach*, Occasional Green Paper No. 8, UK
    Universities Staff Development Unit, Sheffield.

Universal wisdom

Lao Tzu (1963) *Tao Te Ching*, Penguin, London.

—13—

Towards the millennium and beyond

John Doidge, Bob Hardwick and Jenny Wilkinson

The preceding chapters have dealt with a variety of staff development issues which have, in the main, concentrated on the role and professional development of support and allied staff in higher education (HE). This has highlighted their vital contribution to the system as a whole as well as illustrating the importance of induction, appraisal, training and development, team working, qualifications and accreditation. This final chapter therefore concentrates on important developments, as we move towards the millennium. Our main focus will, once again, be the implications for support and allied staff. We hope that this will not be seen as divisive, since there is still too much in HE which seeks to polarize academic and support staff roles. Our main aim throughout has been that our contribution might assist in diminishing and eventually removing any barriers that exist between staff groups, thereby regarding everyone and every contribution as professional. As Sir Ron Dearing recommended in his recent report on HE, institutions 'should identify and remove any barriers which inhibit recruitment and progression for particular groups and monitor and publish their progress towards greater equality of opportunity for all groups'. We hope it will help to shift the glass ceiling faced by a growing number of support and allied staff, impeding their career progression.

For too long we have had the situation where 'once a technician, always a technician' has been the order of the day. This too often applies equally to other support and allied staff. The seed change needed to reverse this trend will only be brought about if it secures the support of senior management and the recognized trade unions. Each could play a key part in this. Indeed, should the current confused national bargaining situation lead eventually to a single spine salary structure, then the mechanism would be in place to allow the kind of career progression that has so far been almost impossible to achieve. The inevitable consequence of this situation led Sir Ron to declare, 'There is concern among staff that they have received neither the recognition, opportunities for personal development, nor the reward which their contribution over the last decade merits.'

Over that decade, change has probably been the most consistent feature in HE and it is not difficult to predict that this will remain the case for the next decade. As the Dearing Report concludes, 'To support and prepare staff for these new working patterns, more focused and appropriate training and staff development activities will be needed.' This will put an additional onus on training and development staff, who are already hard pressed to meet the current demands in many institutions, and on resources for staff development generally. We hope that this book might well serve as a useful source of information. For support and allied staff will, more than ever, be reliant on the support of colleagues, of organizations such as the Universities' and Colleges' Staff Development Agency (UCoSDA) and the vital support gained through network groups.

Supporting staff development through networks

One of UCoSDA's first initiatives, when it was established in 1989, was to organize a UK-wide conference for training and development staff from within HE. This has become an annual event and the ninth conference takes place in November 1997. The theme for the 1997 conference is 'Higher Education into the Future: Implications for Staff Development'. It will specifically consider the findings of the National Committee of Inquiry into Higher Education (the Dearing Report). However, whilst this will be the main focus of the three-day event, the real benefit is that it provides an annual opportunity for HE training and development staff to network with one another. Alongside the usual key note contributions and a series of workshops, time is allocated for special interest groups, allowing delegates to link up with colleagues to discuss issues of common interest and concern. This has in the past led to a number of collaborative projects, closer liaisons, network groups, etc and has, on more than one occasion, prevented the re-inventing of the wheel.

This annual event is augmented by a variety of arrangements at regional level in England and nationally in Scotland, Wales and Ireland. National and regional committees are the most common networks used by the staff development community and these provide the opportunity, on a regular basis, for staff trainers and developers to meet in order to discuss topical issues, areas of common interest, personal development, current concerns, regional collaboration and programmes and institutional initiatives. These committees or groups are constituted in a variety of formats, ranging from the very informal, to the Scottish model where the staff development committee is a sub-group established by Scotland's University and College Principals. The remits of these groups also differ, some concentrating on a particular staff group or subject area, others meeting primarily to share ideas and experiences, whilst some of the committees actually organize their own programme of training and development courses.

These programmes have the advantage of allowing staff from different institutions to meet up and, within the context of the course, share a range of issues with colleagues. One of the outcomes of these programmes can be the establishment of a network, covering some or all of the course participants. The networks are often maintained through e-mail so that information can quickly be relayed between both individuals and groups of network subscribers. This mode of communication is becoming more available to support and allied staff in HE and lends itself to specific or specialist groups of staff. There are already a number of well established e-mail lists and they currently include both subject areas and staff groupings. As a cautionary note, quite large numbers of HE staff still do not have access to this means of communication and, in any case, it is doubtful if its growing usage should replace face-to-face meetings or discussions completely. As one secretary revealed recently, 'My boss communicates by sending me e-mails', and when asked whether this constituted a problem her response was, 'It does when you share the same office.'

Electronic mail does have the obvious advantage when communication has to take place at a distance and can be demonstrated to have some extremely tangible benefits. The technical superintendents network is a good example of this, allowing e-mail messages to be quickly relayed to all subscribing technicians, UK-wide. Other groups using such networks include staff trainers and developers, senior secretarial staff, IT personnel, subject networks, special interest and professional groups, teachers and researchers. The proliferation of these networks is taking place at local, regional and national levels but there is probably scope for even more since we still hear of staff who have no contact mechanisms with others and appear to miss out on learning opportunities.

Towards a learning society

We have decided to conclude this book by taking a brief look at the concept of lifelong learning, a term referred to frequently in a number of chapters. Once again it is appropriate to make reference to the Dearing Report, which is entitled *Higher Education in the Learning Society*. The report began by commenting that:

> Over the next 20 years the United Kingdom must create a society committed to learning throughout life. That commitment will be required from individuals, the state, employers and the providers of education and training. Education is life enriching and desirable in its own right. It is fundamental to an improving quality of life in the UK.

It could be argued that HE should start by putting its own house in order and recognizing that as leaders in the field of education and training for UK and overseas students it has the capability of offering a lot more to its own staff. As Partington (1994) ironically concluded:

> The *raison d'être* of higher education institutions is to provide learning communities for all engaged with them ... the majority of universities and colleges have some way to go, however, in establishing adequately resourced, strategically planned development and training opportunities for *all* staff, in such a way that they could genuinely claim to be, as well as to provide, learning communities.

HE institutions will clearly have to adapt and change quickly in the next few years, resulting in further challenges which will have to met by all staff. As Dearing reflects,

> In becoming more effective, in taking on additional new roles and becoming even more responsive to change, HEIs are necessarily becoming learning organisations with a capacity for adaptation and development which runs throughout the institution. Many respondents insist that all staff have to be brought into such thinking and strategies.

This is probably the first time that such an unambiguous reference has been made to such a major cultural change for many HEIs. We welcome this approach and believe appropriate continuing professional development programmes for all staff can only enhance HE's credibility and ability as providers of learning.

References

Dearing, Sir R (1997) *Higher Education in the Learning Society*, Report of the National Committee of Inquiry in Higher Education.

Partington, PA *et al.* (1994) *Continuing Professional Development (CPD) for Staff in Higher Education: Informing Strategic Thinking*, Occasional Green Paper no. 10, UCoSDA, Sheffield.

Glossary

AAU	Academic Audit Unit
AMP	Academic Management Programme
APEL	Accreditation of Prior Experiential Learning
APL	Accredited Prior Learning
AUA	Association of University Administrators
BPR	Business Process Re-engineering
CAT	Credit Accumulation Transfer
CBI	Confederation of British Industry
CCTV	Closed Circuit Television
ComCon	Educational Competences Consortium
COSHEP	Committee of Scottish Higher Education Principals
COSHH	Control of Substances Hazardous to Health
CPD	Continuing Professional Development
CSUP	Committee of Scottish University Principals
CUA	Conference of University Administrators
CVCP	Committee of Vice-Chancellors and Principals
DFEE	Department for Education and Employment
DMS	Diploma in Management Studies
DTP	Desktop Publishing
ESRC	Economic and Social Research Council
GSP	Graduate Standards Programme
HE	Higher Education
HEFC	Higher Education Funding Council
HEFCE	Higher Education Funding Council England
HEI	Higher Education Institute
HELB	Higher Education Lead Body
HEQC	Higher Education Quality Council
HERA	Higher Education Role Analysis
HESA	Higher Education Statistics Agency
IIP	Investors in People
IS	Information Systems
IT	Information Technology
ITD	Institute of Training and Development
LEC	Local Enterprise Company
MBA	Master of Business Administration
MCI	Management Charter Initiative

MSF	Manufacturing, Science and Finance Union
NTTF	National Training Task Force
NTU	Nottingham Trent University
NVQ	National Vocational Qualification
OECD	Organisation for Economic Co-operation and Development
OSSN	Office Support Staff Network
PCFC	Polytechnics and Colleges Funding Council
PDHE	Professional Development in Higher Education
SCAMAD	Standing Conference on Accreditation and Administration Development
SEDA	Staff and Educational Development Association
SVQ	Scottish Vocational Qualification
SWOT	Strengths, Weaknesses, Opportunities and Threats
TDLB	Training and Development Lead Body
TEC	Training and Enterprise Council
TQM	Total Quality Management
TUC	Trades Union Congress
UCEA	Universities and Colleges Employers Association
UCoSDA	Universities' and Colleges' Staff Development Agency
VQ	Vocational Qualification

Index